Ditch the Pitch!

Digital-Free Client Attraction
Guide for Hypnotists

Wendie Webber

Ditch the Pitch! *Digital-Free Client Attraction Guide for Hypnotists*

Wendie Webber

Copyright © 2025 Wendie Webber
All Rights Reserved.

All rights reserved. No part of this publication may be reproduced, distributed, or transmitted in any form or by any means, including photocopying, recording, or other electronic or mechanical methods without the prior written permission from the author, except in the case of brief quotations embodied in critical reviews and certain non-commercial uses permitted by copyright law.

The information given in this book should not be treated as a substitute for professional medical advice; always consult a medical practitioner. Any use of information in this book is at the reader's discretion and risk. Neither the author nor the publisher can be held responsible for any loss, claim, or damage arising out of the use, or misuse, of the suggestions made, the failure to take medical advice, or for any material on third-party websites.

ISBN Print Book: 978-1-0688514-4-5

What's Inside?

CHAPTER 1: Avoid My Mistakes 7
   Mistake #1 – Selling the Session 8
   Mistake #2 – Casting a Wide Net 9
   Mistake #3 – Making it About "The Hypnosis" 10
   What Do People Know About Hypnosis? 11
   Who? What? How? 13
   Mistake #4 – Menu Marketing 15

CHAPTER 2: Deliver a Clear Message 19
   Turn Callers into Cash 21
   Social Gatherings 27
   Free Consultation 29
   Qualify Your Clients 30
   How Much? 33
   Three Essential Truths of Hypnosis 34

CHAPTER 3: Present Yourself 37
   One-Hour Presentation 39

CHAPTER 4: Teach Self-Hypnosis Classes 49
   Results Will Get You Referrals 51
   The Sweet Spot 52
   An Affordable Option 53
   Convert to Private Sessions 54
   Get Paid More 56

    The Value is Obvious 56

    Self-Hypnosis Class Outline 58

    Make success easy! 61

    Stay in Touch 64

    Facilitate Groups 65

CHAPTER 5: Get Organized 69

CHAPTER 6: Meet People 89

    It's Your Business 92

CHAPTER 7: Get Compensated Fairly 95

    Session Packages 97

    Coupon Deals 98

    Think Before You Act 100

CHAPTER 8: Get Great Testimonials 105

    The Best Testimonials 106

    How to Get Great Testimonials 107

    Answer the Burning Questions 118

CHAPTER 9: Get Started – Get Paid 121

    Conduct a Study 122

CHAPTER 10: Keep in Contact 129

    A Relationship Based on Trust 130

    Maintain the Relationship 131

    Create a Referral Program 133

CHAPTER 11: Grow Your Business 135

    Hypnosis Practice Business System 136

    An Integrated Practice-Business System 149

WHY READ THIS BOOK

I don't like marketing. Most therapists don't like marketing. It doesn't feel authentic or truthful, it feels like *selling*. We're not salespeople, we're healers, for gawd-sake! We just want to help people! As a result, self-promoting makes us feel uncomfortable. And what do you do when you feel uncomfortable? *Avoid*, of course. It's only natural to want to avoid the things we don't like. But marketing is how you get clients. If you don't get clients, you're going to struggle to make a living. Marketing is how you attract paying clients into your practice. What I failed to recognize is that client attraction isn't about getting "more" clients. "More" clients just mean more problems to deal with in your sessions. And when you're just starting out you don't need more problems. You need some wins! That's what will help you to increase your confidence.

Healing isn't merely a way for you to make a living – it's a calling. But too many heart-centered healers are struggling. They're struggling with how to take everything they learned in the classroom and use it to get consistent results working with real clients in the session room. As a result, they're struggling with their confidence. And they're struggling with how to get enough clients to make a living. Whether you're a seasoned practitioner with years of experience, or just starting out, your most important asset in the session room is always going to be your confidence. But when you're just starting out, you can waste a lot of time and money trying to figure it all out on your own. (I know I did.)

I decided to write this book for you because I know what it's like to struggle with lack of confidence coupled with the need to attract clients. It took me *far too long* to figure things out. In the process, I made a lot of costly mistakes. You won't have to.

I want to save you the time and frustration that comes with trial-and-error learning. What I am about to share with you are simple strategies you can use right away to attract the right kinds of clients into your healing services – the ones you can be successful with. That's how you'll grow your confidence.

If you're a hypnotherapist who doesn't love marketing, and you want some simple, proven strategies you can use to promote yourself and your services *without* being harnessed to the artificial world of digital technology, you're in the right place. **Ditch the Pitch!** is a beginner's guide to marketing yourself and your services *without* having to do that dreaded sales pitch, figure out how to game the algorithms on social media, or stay on top of SEO. This is an old-school, hands-on approach for healers who want to take care of business by connecting with real people who truly need your help. That's it.

I'm also going to point out some of the things they don't teach you in hypnosis school. I invested well over 1,500 hours in classroom time learning how to get real results working with real clients. Not one of those courses ever showed me how to get paid for doing that. In fact, it wasn't until I started learning how to set up and grow a *digital* business that I made an unsettling realization; there are two sides to any healing practice. On the one hand, you have the practice of hypnosis. On the other hand, there's the business. If you neglect one side, you'll struggle to make a living.

The practice side is what attracted you to the healing profession. It involves everything you were taught in hypnosis school. It's about how to use your inductions, deepeners, and therapeutic techniques to get the desired result for your clients. These therapeutic tools and techniques empower you to make a real difference in a person's life. But too many hypnosis practitioners end up focused on trying to get the next client just so they can pay the next bill. As a result, their business strategy ends up looking something like this:

1. Get a client.
2. Do the hypnosis.
3. Get paid.
4. Find the next client.

Do you know what that is? It's a rut. You spend all your time chasing money instead of fulfilling the dream that called you to hypnosis in the first place. That's no way to make a living.

You really can help a person transform their lives from the inside out by changing how they think and feel – about themselves, others, and life. But if you want to *make a living* doing that, you need to take care of the business. The business side is what supports you in getting *paid*. When you work for yourself, you are also a *business owner*. It's up to you to take care of the business. Business is about making money.

To make a living as a healing practitioner, you need to develop your expertise in *business*. Clients equals cash. No clients = no cash. If you have a background in business, then you probably already know something about marketing and promotion. This means that you have some transferable skills which can be applied to your healing practice. But if you don't know anything about business, you need to be prepared to invest in learning how to run the business end of things. That includes marketing.

Hypnosis Practice Business System

It turns out that the system that took me years to figure out isn't new. It's grounded in solid, proven business principles that work. Not only did this help me to get more consistent results working with real clients with real problems, but it also helped me to get paid a premium fee by offering a premium service. It can help you, too.

The system I will share with you isn't complex. It's a simple blueprint - so simple you could draw it on a napkin - but it contains all the key elements you need to set up and grow a thriving healing practice. These are the things that I wish I had known when I was first starting out. It would have saved me a ton of time and money.

I invested well over a decade studying hypnosis and I was never taught any of this. What I'm about to share with you can help you to:

- ✓ Get more clients you can be successful with
- ✓ Feel more confident in your healing sessions
- ✓ Get more consistent/lasting results with your clients
- ✓ Make a lot more money with a lot less work

In Chapter 1, I'll share some of the costly marketing mistakes that I made - so you can avoid them. You'll also learn how to formulate a clear marketing message that you can use everywhere.

In Chapter 2, we'll look at three essential truths about hypnosis that can get you into trouble, and how you can take advantage of a free consultation to get more clients.

In Chapter 3, you'll learn how to get more clients by educating the public about what you do by giving presentations. You'll also learn how to structure a one-hour presentation.

In Chapter 4, you'll learn how you can make more money by teaching self-hypnosis classes. This includes an outline of how you can structure a one or two-day class, and how to convert your students into private sessions.

In Chapter 5, I'll share some tips on how to make your presentations more engaging.

In Chapter 6, we'll look at how meeting people at events such as holistic fears can help you to get more students and clients.

In Chapter 7, we'll look at how to ensure you're being fairly compensated for your services. Included are some common disasters associated with discounting services and how it might be to benefit from offering a coupon deal.

In Chapter 8, we'll explore the mistakes and benefits of client testimonials; how to get them, and how to use them more effectively.

In Chapter 9, I'll share a simple strategy you can use to increase your confidence by facilitating multiple sessions without any pressure to produce a result.

In Chapter 101, we'll look at the importance of staying in touch with your students and clients, and how you can create a referral program.

In chapter 11, we'll look at how having systems in place can support you in doing your best work while also helping you to grow your business. I'll share a simple five-step blueprint for a system that works. Start using it right away and you'll simplify the business side of things, allowing you to focus more on what truly matters – helping your clients to heal.

Ready?

Read on . . .

CHAPTER 1:
Avoid My Mistakes

People don't pay for hypnosis. They pay for the results. They're paying you to help them to lose weight, break the unwanted habit, heal the relationship, and put an end to the pain. Deliver on your promise of results *consistently* and you can build a referral-based business. Your results will give you satisfied clients who trust you. They'll come back to work on other issues. And they'll send you more clients. That's the easiest way to grow your healing practice. What's more, your reputation as an expert hypnotherapist and trusted healing guide will allow you to charge a premium fee for your services. People will gladly pay a premium fee if you can help them get rid of the problem *for good*.

It turns out the secret to growing a thriving healing practice is no secret, at all. It isn't in clever advertising or how pretty your website is. Those things are nice, but they won't help if you can't deliver on your promise of results. That's where the rubber meets the road.

Mistake #1 – Selling the Session

My Big Fat Marketing Mistake #1 was thinking, "marketing is sales". It's not. Marketing is simply whatever you do to attract clients to you. It's your "client attraction system." Marketing is how you communicate about what you do and how you can help people.

The *purpose* of your marketing is to attract the right kinds of people to you. These are the clients you can be most successful with, and who will benefit the most from what you have to offer. They're also the people you'll love to work with most. Client attraction is about making sure you're getting the right clients *for you* because that's what will ensure your best results. Your results will bring you more clients.

Now think about this; *everybody's got a story*. For most people that story has some pain in it. It's their Pain Story. This means that, no matter who you meet, they are potentially your client because, deep down inside, they've got some kind of problem that their subconscious mind has been working on, 24/7, trying to find a solution for.

When a person thinks or feels or acts in ways that they don't like, it's because there's an underlying problem that their conscious mind doesn't know about, doesn't *want* to know about, or just can't fix. That's because the conscious mind doesn't have the whole story. All it can do is apply reason and logic to try to make sense of the problem. When that doesn't work, it comes up with excuses for having the problem. While this can provide a much-needed sense of control, it fails to get rid of the problem. That's when unwanted behaviors can be adopted as coping strategies, or to avoid the pain of the problem, which only makes things worse.

The problem might be physical, emotional, or spiritual in nature, but when a problem is rooted in the subconscious mind – that's where we work! *You* are uniquely qualified to gain access to *that* story. Then, you can help the client find a lasting solution to the problem. Don't you think people would love to know that about you? All you need is the opportunity to have a conversation with them. That's it.

It's not about trying to sell them anything. It's about inviting a conversation. It's about gaining permission to get to know that person better. It's about helping them to feel comfortable enough to tell you their Pain Story.

Mistake #2 – Casting a Wide Net

My second big fat marketing mistake was not being specific enough. I thought, "Cast a wide net, you'll get more fish!" Wrong. If you try to get everybody, you're going to get nobody. You need to zero-in on that "one person" who is an ideal fit for you and speak to them. Not the crowd. Not the masses. Just that one person.

The secret to effectively marketing yourself is not trying to be all things to all people. It's in having a clear message that speaks to that one person, your ideal client. Be very specific about who your ideal client is, what their specific issue is, and the benefits of the change that they want. This shows that you "get" them. When a person reads your promotional material or hears you speak, they'll recognize themselves. They'll think, "Hey, that's me!" That's when something wonderful happens. They begin to feel a sort of kinship with you. That's when they'll start paying attention to what you have to say.

When a person reads your marketing message, or hears you speak, they should also get a sense of who *you* are and how you might be the best choice for *them*. That's important because people need to feel that they know you, like you, and trust you before they buy from you.

The goal is to weed out the ones that aren't a good match. Remember, you don't need more clients. You need clients you can be successful with! If they are a good match, and it seems to them like you might have the solution they've been looking for, they're going to want to hear more. That's when they'll pick up the phone and call you.

This is the fundamental purpose of marketing. It's not to try to sell the session. It's to attract your ideal client and *get them to call you*. I hope you can appreciate how much simpler this makes things for you. All you need to do is clearly communicate about the one thing you most love - helping a specific person get free of a specific problem they have been struggling with. Then, once you have a clear message, you can then carry it into all your promotional material.

Mistake #3 – Making it About "The Hypnosis"

When a person asks you, "What do you do?", how do you think you should respond? The *last* thing you ever want to say is, "I'm a hypnotist." Why? Because that response might not get a conversation with them.

My third marketing mistake was trying to market "the hypnosis." I had been so steeped in the "hypnosis is the answer" theology that I didn't realize I was avoiding promoting *myself*. That's what happens when you don't feel confident in the session room. It makes it hard to speak with conviction about what you do because you don't believe in yourself. So, what do you do? You talk about the power of hypnosis, instead. You talk about what's possible with hypnosis. The problem with marketing "the hypnosis" is that nobody cares about hypnosis. Most people don't know anything about hypnosis. Why would they care about it? It's *your* job to care about the hypnosis and use it in a way that will help them out of the problem.

What Do People Know About Hypnosis?

When it comes to hypnosis, there are basically three kinds of people.

1. People who *don't know* anything about hypnosis.
2. People who *think* they know what hypnosis is.
3. People who *know* what it is (and it ain't good.)

They Don't Know Anything: If they *don't know* anything about hypnosis, and you're lucky, they might be curious enough to want to learn more. But a lot of people are afraid of looking stupid. If they don't know anything about hypnosis, they might just change the subject or do something to avoid. The result? You won't get the conversation.

They Think They Know: If they *think they know* what hypnosis is, most of the time it's based on stage hypnosis or Hollywood. In this case, what they know is that you can control them and make them bark like a chicken. Right? They may not even want to look you in the eye, which makes it very difficult to have a conversation. You need to throw out the welcome mat and make a person feel comfortable with you. The goal is to pique their curiosity and so they'll ask, "Tell me more!"

Most people are naturally curious. Even if they *don't* know a thing about hypnosis, or *think* they know, they'll still be open to learning from you. See if you can entice them to *ask* you about what you do and how you help.

They Know (and it ain't good): When a person knows what hypnosis is because they had a bad experience with it in the past, *if you're lucky*, they'll tell you about their experience. This will then give you the opportunity to change their mind about hypnosis. The key is to stay curious and be open to hearing their story.

I have had clients tell me they would *never* do hypnosis because they'd been dumped into a traumatic event by an unskilled hypnotist or psychologist, and it hadn't gone well. I just made it my mission to change their mind because they were still struggling with the problem. As a result, I learned something very important from these clients. I learned that just because a person has had a "bad" experience with hypnosis in the past does not mean they will be a "bad" or "resistant" client. Some of my best clients have been members of the "hypnosis never again" club!

Remember, nobody cares about hypnosis. They don't care about you. People are primarily interested in themselves – their health, wealth, happiness, work, relationships, children – and what's going on in their lives. Some people may be intrigued by hypnosis. But don't count on it. Many people will just feel intimidated by it. They'll be afraid of your powers to control them. They may not admit it, but they won't want to even look you in the eye! But everybody has a Pain Story. That's where you need to focus. Focus on the pain of the problem because the only thing they're interested in is - *can you help them to get unstuck?*

They don't care about your tools or techniques, either. Or what school you graduated from. Or who you studied under. Some people may be attracted to a particular technique if they know someone who was helped by it. But the tool isn't the answer they're looking for. *You* are. They just don't know it, yet.

Who? What? How?

Who is your ideal client? Who is that "one person" that comes to mind when you think of your dream client? You know, the one you just love to work with? Who is that one person you with all your clients were like? What makes this person an ideal match for you?

What's the problem? What has them worried? What is it that's keeping them awake at night? Think about the pain, the shame, the guilt, the fear, the frustration, the anger it's been causing them. What specific issue do you most love to work with? What problem has the most heart for you? What are you most knowledgeable about? What are you most interested in learning more about? Focus on *that*.

Human beings are naturally hard-wired to seek pleasure and avoid pain. That's their WIIFM - what's in it for me? What do they want instead? What does relief look like for them? What is it that they want so much they would gladly pay money to get it? The relief? The control? The freedom? These are the benefits of change. How can you help them to get that? How do *you* have the answer to moving them out of pain and into having the benefits they long for?

How are you the answer for that person with that problem? Not the hypnosis, not the technique, YOU. Can you help them to get rid of the problem? That's all they care about. Can you get them out of that awful somebody-done-somebody-wrong song they've been singing to themselves, over and over again, in the privacy of their own mind? What is it about this specific problem that you understand so well that it makes you the obvious choice? What do you know that they don't know? What makes you the *best choice* for that person?

Put these all together and you have everything you need to craft an effective Who-What-How Statement. WHO do you help? WHAT do you help them with? HOW can they benefit from working with you? For example: "I help women who are emotional over-eaters get back in control of their eating habits . . . so they can get slim and trim and feel good about themselves."

Some people call this their "elevator spiel." The idea is to know what to say if you ever find yourself in an elevator, or a waiting room, or at a social gathering, and someone asks, "What do you do?" Having a well-formulated Who-What-How statement ready will ensure you won't make the mistake of saying those three deadly words that can kill any conversation - "I'm a hypnotist."

A moving company doesn't tell you about what kind of trucks they drive. They tell you how they are experts at moving your stuff from where you're currently at to where you want to be. They tell you how they will do that in the most safe and expedient manner. You need to be like the moving company and offer the right solution to the right person.

Who? Women who can't control their eating. What? The problem of emotional over-eating. How? You can help them get back in control, look good, and feel good about themselves. Isn't that more attractive than, "I'm a hypnotist"?

Engaging with people authentically is what will make you a client magnet. Not only will this help you to feel more confident promoting yourself, but it will also give you many more opportunities to connect with the kinds of people you can be successful with.

When you speak to the specific issue that a person has been struggling with you are singing their song! The trick is to focus on what you're most passionate about. That's where your energy is. Then, just offer enough information to pique a person's interest. Remember, your goal is not to try to sell them a session. It is simply to get them to say, "Really? Tell me more." When that happens, you have just successfully marketed yourself!

Mistake #4 – Menu Marketing

Menu marketing is where you offer a list of all the issues hypnosis has been shown to be effective at resolving. The main problem with this approach is that it's not specific enough to grab anyone's attention. Unfortunately, too many hypnosis practitioners employ this strategy because they're afraid of missing out. Do you recognize Mistake #2 here? "Cast a wide net, you'll get more fish!" It doesn't work because you're not speaking to anyone in particular! Worse, if you are perceived as a jack-of-all-trades, you'll be regarded as a master-of-none. Don't be a "Jack!"

I wish I had known all this years ago. It would have saved me so much frustration, not to mention a ton of money.

Remember, *everybody* has a problem. You just need to pick one. Ideally, pick a specific issue that interests you, that you're good at, that you want to learn more about. The truth is that you can't help everyone. Besides, you don't *want* to work with just anybody. You want clients you can be successful with. Think of it this way . . . In a hypnosis session you're marketing to a person's subconscious mind. You're speaking to the part of the mind that causes the client to feel the way they feel. When you focus on a specific problem and how much pain it's causing that person, you are focusing their attention on something they feel is important. You are speaking directly to the feeling part of their mind and it's saying, "Yah, you *get* me!" That's when the subconscious mind opens to hearing what you have to say.

If you want a person to listen to you, speak to their specific issue. Generalities just aren't personal enough to get anyone's attention. This is why generic scripts don't work very well. You must speak directly to WHO the client is, and WHAT their specific problem is. And if you want to make progress working with *any* client, you need to focus on one specific issue at a time. You focus on the weight problem, or the smoking problem, or the fear problem. But you never work on all three at once.

Focusing on multiple problems at the same time is like trying to clean every room in the house at the same time. Sure, you can do it, but it takes forever, and your client may give up before the job gets done. You focus on one room at a time because that will get you quicker results. The changes will be more obvious, which will, in turn, will help to motivate your client to move onto the next room by providing proof. Now they now know *it's possible* to feel better. This erases all doubt which makes your job easier.

Plus, you've given your client a measure of success to fall back on. Now they *know* that YOU are the solution.

The same is true when it comes to attracting clients. You won't get great results if you try to speak to a list of problems. If you want people to pick up the phone and call you, you need to be perceived as an expert. You need to grab their attention and, at the same time, stand out from all the other choices available to them.

You won't get great results if you try to speak to thousands of people. Speak to that one person who is the ideal match for you, and you'll grab their attention.

Just as you would in a private session, keep the focus of attention on the pain of the problem. Even if that's not the real problem, you still need to give attention to the specific pain that brought the client into your office because that's what's got their attention. That's their motivating factor - their WIIFM.

Bring their awareness to all the distress they've had to endure. Show that you "get" them by reminding them of just how hard it has been for them. This increases motivation to get rid of the problem. Show that you understand what they're going through, that you care about how it's impacting them in their life. Show them that *you* are the answer they've been looking for and you'll get that conversation. Every time.

Summary:

Remember to avoid these common mistakes:

1. Trying to sell the session.
2. Trying to get everybody.
3. Making it all about the hypnosis.
4. Menu Marketing

Remember, when it comes to hypnosis there are basically three kinds of people.

1. People who *don't know* anything about hypnosis.
2. People who *think* they know what hypnosis is.
3. People who *know* what it is (and it ain't good.)

Remember the Who-What-How formula:

1. Who is your ideal client?
2. What is their problem?
3. How are you the answer for that person with that problem?

CHAPTER 2:
Deliver a Clear Message

Regardless of what a person may think about hypnosis, they'll be receptive to learning more from you if you speak with authority about their specific problem. They'll be interested in learning about what *you* do because your Who-What-How statement isn't about "the hypnosis." It's all about *them*. This makes *you* very attractive.

When someone asks, "What do you do?" your first response should always be, "I'm so glad you asked!" Then, offer them your well-formulated Who-What-How statement. For example, "I help men who are going through a painful marriage breakup heal so they can feel worthy of love again." Or "I help teenagers become academic 'rock-stars' by improving their study skills and helping them overcoming test-anxiety!" Or "I help kids who have a problem with bedwetting wake to a dry bed every morning so they can feel good about themselves . . . and their parents can have peace of mind (and finally get a good night's sleep!)"

Okay, maybe these don't speak specifically to what *you* care most about or want to do, but I hope you get the idea. WHO do you help? WHAT do you help them with? HOW will they benefit from working with you to resolve that problem?

Having a clear marketing message will get you more conversations with more people - which will get you more clients. More importantly, it will get you more of the right kinds of clients. The key is to stick to your script and communicate in a way that is authentic and true for *you*. Even when the person you're speaking to doesn't have that specific issue, you still might capture their interest. They'll want to know more because they know someone who *has* that problem. Or they might be wondering if you could help them with a problem they *do* have. Either way, it opens the door to having a conversation.

They may not be the parents of school-aged children, but maybe they are grandparents. Maybe it's a *woman* who is going through a bitter divorce who could really benefit from some emotional healing and support. Maybe it's a *man* who doesn't feel good about himself because he's packed on a few pounds. Do you know what will happen? They'll ask, "Do you work with *women* going through divorce?" "Do you work with *adults* with test anxiety?" "Do you offer weight loss programs to men?" What they're really asking is, "Are *you* the answer I have been looking for?"

You *are* the answer – and for a lot more people than you realize. That's why your prime objective should be to spark a person's imagination. That's speaking to their subconscious mind. Tickle their curiosity so that, even if you're not an exact fit for them, they may just find you the most fascinating person on the planet. Do that and the next time they talk to a friend who is going through a divorce, or they meet someone who has an anxious teenager, or a bedwetting six-year-old, they'll remember you. They'll recommend you to them. This is the best kind of marketing money can't buy. It's being recommended to someone by a trusted friend. That's gold.

Turn Callers into Cash

You just don't get a second chance at making a good first impression. You want that first impression to be that *you* are a professional. But you're not always going to be available to answer the phone when a person calls. But not everyone will call back if you don't pick up the phone. They'll just move on and call somebody else. Some people can be put off by the fact that you weren't sitting on the phone waiting for their call. I know it seems silly. But the problem is that they've been sitting on the problem for too long. When they finally decide to pick up the phone, and there's nobody there to take their call, they move on. People who are stressed out with a problem aren't always thinking straight. They may just bail out if you don't give them a good reason to leave you a message.

You can establish rapport with a person, even when you're not speaking with them in person. Just record a voicemail message that suggests, "I'm so glad you called!" Then deliver a Who-What-How message. Your voicemail message can then act as a suggestion that delivers a set of instructions by telling your caller *who* you are, *what* action you want them to take, and *why* it's in their best interest to leave you a message.

Begin by telling them who you are. Introduce yourself. Include your business name. For example, "Hi! You have reached Jane Doe of ABC Hypnosis."

Tell them *what* action you want them to take. You want them to leave you their name and call-back number, right? Then tell them *why* they should leave you a message. Remember, you're here to help. Make it reasonable for you not to be sitting on the phone waiting for their call. For example, "I'm either out of the office or working with a client right now." This puts a picture in their head of you helping someone. (And if they had called earlier that "someone" could have been them.)

Make it reasonable for them to leave you their call-back information. For example, "Your call is important to me. At the sound of the tone please leave your name and number. I'll return your call as soon as I'm back in the office." Put it all together and your voicemail message acts as a suggestion to deliver your Who-What-Why message. For example, "Hello, you've reached John Doe of ABC Healing Practice and ABC Healing Hypnosis dot com. I am either out of the office or working with a client right now, so please leave a message. At the sound of the tone remember – *your success is important.* So please leave your name and number. And I'll get back to you as soon as possible."

Make your message relevant to the caller. Speak as you would to a real person. When you promise to return their call make sure you *keep* your promise. Remember, this is their first encounter with you. It could be the beginning of a beautiful relationship. Your message should let the caller know that they matter to you – because they do. Don't put off calling them back for two days. People will forgive you for not being available right away *if* you give them a good reason. But if it seems like you can't be bothered to call them back for a week … well, you know how that feels. When a person calls you the window of opportunity is open today. But it may be closed tomorrow. Check your messages frequently throughout the day. And return your calls as quickly as possible. A prompt follow-up can get you more clients.

The moment you convince a caller to leave you a message you have successfully created the opportunity to have a conversation with them. Any conversation is an opportunity to qualify and schedule in a new client. If they're the right client for you, the next step is to schedule them in for their first session. But before the phone starts ringing, you need to be ready to *have* a conversation. That's where you can convert callers into clients. When a person calls to inquire about your services, you need to be ready to guide the conversation.

There are three things that will support you in guiding a conversation that leads to booking a new client. These are things you should keep close at hand. First, you need a dedicated notebook for phone messages. Second, your day timer or scheduler so you can book the appointment. Third, the following Six Critical Qualifying Questions[1].

Six Critical Qualifying Questions
1. What's the problem?
2. Why is it a problem?
3. How much of a problem is it?
4. What do they know about hypnosis?
5. What questions do they have about the process?
6. How soon would they like to get started?

If you're just starting it can also be helpful to keep a list of frequently asked questions close at hand. This can help you to feel more confident fielding any questions. Your FAQ sheet should be easy to

---

[1] For a deeper dive into how to qualify your clients, get Ditch the Script: *Get Everything You Need from the Client for Successful Hypnotherapy and Set p to Wrap Up with Results*

reference. For example, a list of bullet-point responses. This will empower you to respond confidently to common misperceptions about hypnosis. Also, have your rate schedule available if you offer packages or taxes apply.

During the initial call or consultation there are four key pieces of information to make note of.

1. The caller's name.
2. The date they called.
3. The problem they called you about.
4. Their contact info. (i.e. phone/email)

Even if you have Call Display, make sure to confirm their phone number with them. They may be calling from work or home or somewhere else. Some people don't want you to call them there. It's important to respect their privacy.

During the initial conversation with a person, you're going to answer their questions and address any concerns they might have. But keep in mind, as you're having this conversation, that you're forging the beginning of a relationship. That's what healing hypnosis is – a relationship based in healing. It's a journey you take together with a shared goal of healing.

Treat them *as if* they are ready to get started with you. Be inclusive in your conversation. For example, "Here's what we'll do." "When you come in, here's what will happen." And take good notes during your conversation with the caller. Keeping a notebook is a good habit to develop. If you use a dedicated notebook to record all your phone messages and conversations, you'll have a record of telephone events.

This will ensure that you never have to leave anything to memory. Write it down. That first conversation is the beginning of a relationship. Not every person is going to schedule an appointment with you right away. But they may book a session with you later. You'll need a way to remember them. If they don't book an appointment right away, make a note of where you left things off.

If you agreed to call them later, make sure to schedule yourself a reminder. Then, when it comes time to call them back, all you need to do is pull out your notebook, quickly review your last conversation with them. And you'll be able to pick up where you left off.

When you remember a person who you had a conversation with, weeks or even months later, it helps them to feel heard and important. It shows that you care. If you can "remember" their husband names is Richard, that they're taking care of their ailing mother, Joyce, and that their dog's name is Patches, you're no longer just another business. You've become a trusted friend. That will get you more clients.

As you can see, your notebook can be a source of gold when it comes to getting new clients. It gives you a record of your first contact with a person. It provides you with key information about them so that you'll remember them when you speak again. Some people will tell you things over the phone that they won't mention during the intake process. This might turn out to be information that is critical to their healing.

No Doesn't Mean Never

Sometimes, when a person calls to inquire about your services, they're not ready to proceed with you right away. This is why you keep good notes. I've had clients who were waiting for money to come in. Or they were going away for a week. Or they wanted to wait until they spoke with their doctor. Or they were waiting for the test results.

There may be information a client shares with you that you want to research before their first session. For example, they may tell you certain medications they're taking. Or they may have a diagnosis. This information can help you to prepare yourself before they come in for their first session. You can do a little research to see just what you're dealing with. Recognize that, when a person receives a diagnosis, they accept suggestions from a medical authority about what that diagnosis means. These suggestions are accepted unconsciously. They can impact outcomes. The person may be completely unaware that there are added worries and concerns contributing to the problem. Being informed about their diagnosis can help you to uncover these concerns.

When a person is prescribed medication, there are side-effects. That's what they do. But some medications can be contributing to the symptoms. For example, some medications cause weight gain. Some disrupt sleep. Some medications can affect a person's responses in hypnosis. Some cause drowsiness. Some can even block a person's ability to enter hypnosis. At the very least, it's important to be able to have an intelligent conversation with the client about their issue. This will help them to trust you.

Sometimes there are valid reasons to wait. If the person is not ready to take the next step and begin the healing process, the next step for *you* is to get permission to *continue* the conversation at a later date. Set things up so that you have another opportunity to book the session. Ask, "Would be all right for me to check back in with you?" If so, when would be a good time to call them? For example, if they're seeing their doctor next Thursday, you could schedule an appointment to have another conversation on Friday.

Just because a person says "no" doesn't mean "never." It's just means "not now." Don't just leave it up to them to call you back. If you do – you're leaving too much to chance. Ask permission to call them. Most people will appreciate you taking charge on their behalf. And getting permission to call a person back just gives you another kick at the can. It's another opportunity for you to schedule in a new client.

Once you get the booked in for their first session, you can transfer that information into your client file. Both your client-file and call notes serve the same purpose: to keep a record of your interactions with the client. Keep a dedicated notebook for recording calls. Then treat your call book as you would session notes. The information you gather during the initial conversation will be relevant to the client's healing.

Social Gatherings

If you're at a social gathering such as a networking event, a workshop, or a dinner party, and the person you're talking with mentions that they have a particular problem, pay attention. They may just be ready to become your next client. The fact that they have mentioned they have a problem tells you one thing - they're interested in what you do and they're wondering whether you can help them! They may not tell you this but secretly they're wondering – "Are *you* the answer I've been looking for?"

You definitely want to have a conversation with this person. But in a social situation the purpose of the conversation is not to schedule them in for a session. It's to casually assess whether they might be the right client for you.

It's simply *not* in your best interest to try to sell a person something they don't want or need. Or that they're not ready for. All that will get you are problems in sessions that you're not prepared for. Not only can this cost you your confidence, but it also won't get you the results you want.

Don't stand off in the corner pouring over their life history. That could cost you a half-dozen *other* conversations you could be having that could get you more clients. The place for an in-depth conversation about a prospective client's issue is in the privacy of your office. That conversation could take place in person, or over the phone, but it requires a more intimate setting. These things must be handled delicately, right? If the person you're conversing with is open to having a more intimate conversation with you about their issue, you have just attracted a potential new client. Well done!

The next step is to make sure that you *get* that call. Don't leave things to chance. Don't just hand them your card and leave it up to them to call you. Chances are, they won't. Life happens, people get distracted, and there's a good chance they'll forget about you. It's not personal. You just need to take charge and make sure that you get the conversation. The way to do that is to *ask* for it. Ask permission to call *them*. Get their phone number. Then, find out when would be a convenient time for you to call[2]. If possible, schedule the call with them. Make an appointment to have a more in-depth conversation with them.

---

[2] Some people do not want their spouse to know that they're seeing a hypnotherapist. Respect their need for privacy.

Free Consultation

Offering a free consultation is a smart marketing strategy that can get more people to call you. The more callers you can attract, the more opportunities you'll have to book more clients. This is something that you can offer in person, on your website, and through any of your marketing material. A free consultation gives you a way to have a more intimate conversation with a potential client. It also gives you the opportunity to assess whether that person is the right client for you. If they are, you can convert that conversation into a new client by booking the first session.

There's no cost, no obligation, and no risk. This makes it safe for a person to pick up the phone to call you. Remember, the subconscious mind's Prime Directive is safety! That's who you're marketing to. You can call it a "discovery call" or a "preliminary consultation" or an "assessment call." Whatever sounds the most authentic for you.

Let your prospective clients know what will happen when they have that more in-depth conversation with you. Be clear - it's not a session. It's just a friendly chat in a more appropriate (private) setting where you can learn more about the problem they're dealing with. This conversation should give you a better idea of what might be the best approach for them, and you can answer any questions they might have about the process. If it seems like you might be a good fit for one another, they can then decide how they'd like to proceed with you.

You can conduct a free consultation over the phone or in your office. But this is important. Limit the conversation to 15 or 20 minutes. Don't turn it into a free session. The purpose of a free consultation should be to qualify your clients. A 20-minute consultation over the phone or in the office is plenty of time to do that. Remember, you don't need "more" clients. You need the right kind of clients - the ones that will give you the best success rate possible.

Qualify Your Clients

Every successful hypnotherapist knows how important it is to assess a person before accepting them as a client. If you don't, you could end up working much harder than you need to, and you might not get the results you're after. Qualifying your clients will give you a much higher success rate in your sessions by letting both you and the client know what you're getting yourselves into.

In **The Devil's Therapy**[3] I used Grimm's Fairy Tale, the Devil's Grimy Brother, to illustrate the whole healing process of regression hypnosis. The Story begins with a soldier who has been discharged from the army. And he's struggling. He hasn't any money. He doesn't know what to do. He's tried everything. Eventually he wanders into the woods. There he meets a little man who turns out to be, you guessed it, the devil. Like you, the guy in the woods is a fringe-dweller. He's not mainstream. He's offering an unconventional approach to healing. Heck, in some parts of the world, hypnosis is still considered the work of the devil.

The *soldier* is your typical client. He's someone who's been struggling with a problem. He's tried everything. Nothing else has worked. And he's thinking, "Maybe, just maybe, hypnosis can help." That's when they wander into your office. When that happens, the devil asks a very important, two-part question. "He asks, "What's wrong?" And "Why

---

[3] The Devil's Therapy: *Hypnosis Practitioner's Essential Guide to Effective Regression Hypnotherapy*

do you look so unhappy?" This is so juicy. The first part of the question is - What's the problem? This speaks to the reason the person is calling you. Whatever they're dealing with, they think *that's the problem*.

The conversation needs to be about the client - not the hypnosis. If you're going to help them, you need to establish a relationship. Get them talking about the problem. This opens the door to the second part of the question is, "Why do you look so *unhappy*?" This points to the real problem. "Unhappy" is an *emotional* problem. The subconscious mind is the emotional mind. That's where we work.

The real problem is how the person *looks* at things. This points to a problem of perception. How you look at things is how you picture them in your mind. That's what a thought is. It's how a person pictures things mentally. Negative thoughts generate unhappy feelings. Another word for "unhappy" is dis-ease. Dis-ease is essentially a state of unhappiness – physically, mentally, or emotionally. The devil nailed it! The way we picture anything has everything to do with our past experiences.

This is what the work of regression hypnotherapy is all about. It's not about changing past events. It's about changing how a person thinks and feels *because* of past events. Changing how a person looks at things changes everything. It changes how they think, and feel, and behave. It changes how they see themselves and others, and how they respond to situations in daily life. That's pretty much sums up everything you work with, right?

The fact that a problem has been around for a while can work in your favor. There's more pressure which means more dis-ease. That can increase the client's motivation to resolve the problem and get some relief. But it also means the underlying problem has had time to grow and fester and invite a few of its friends over. This can add complexity. Complex issues can take time because you're no longer dealing with a simple issue. To get a lasting result you need to resolve all the contributing factors. That can take time.

Most people don't know this. Most people are just looking for a quick fix. That's understandable. After all, we have all been conditioned to take a pill to make the pain go away. But the pill is only ever a temporary fix. Unresolved problems tend to get worse over time. That's when people turn to hypnosis for help. When external solutions fail and the pressure gets to be too much, that's when most people consider hypnotherapy.

Of course, they want you to make it all go away in a single session. *Of course,* they don't want to throw another dollar at this persistent problem. But hypnotherapy isn't about rotating the tires. Or tuning up the muffler bearings. It's about changing the mind.

When a person has been struggling with a problem for a long time, decades sometimes, it's not reasonable to expect to get rid of it in a couple of hours. Yes, it's possible. But the one-session-miracle is an exception, not the rule. Treat the symptoms and you'll get temporary results. Address the underlying root cause of the problem and you can pull the roots out completely. That will get you a lasting result. The question is- what do they want? A quick fix with a short shelf life? Or a long-term resolution of the *real* problem? Most people want the problem to be gone for good. It's best to dispel the quick-fix mentality before you schedule the first session.

How Much?

When a person calls to inquire about your services, most of the time the first question they're going to ask, "how much?" You do not want to answer that question. At least, not right away. It's a common mistake. After all, when you're just starting out, you just want to get warm bodies into your hypnosis chair so that you can use all your shiny new tools. You first need to qualify the client. If you don't, you're going to have problems in your sessions. You could find yourself in over your head in sessions or struggling to get a result. That could cost you your greatest asset in a session - your confidence.

You need to feel confident in your sessions to feel confident enough to go out and promote yourself and your services! So really get this – you can't be all things to all people. Don't even try. You can't afford to work with just anyone. You need clients you can be successful with. When a person asks you, "How much?" or "How many sessions?" realize it's too soon to be discussing your fee.

Instead, take charge of the conversation by responding, "I'm very happy to answer all your questions. Would it be alright if I ask *you* a few questions, first?" Then, guide the conversation in a way that allows you to assess whether they're the right client for you.

The place to begin is by inviting the person to tell you about the problem they're dealing with. That's their reason for calling. They took the time to pick up the phone and call you because they have a problem they can't fix. They *know* they need help with it. But they're *shopping* for a solution. You may just be the answer they've been looking for. But you need to help them to feel comfortable talking with you about themselves and the problem.

Remember, you don't know this person. They don't know you. The purpose of the call is to get to know each other because therapeutic hypnosis requires a relationship. That's what you're qualifying a person for – a *therapeutic relationship.*

Another question a person might ask is, "*How many sessions?*" It's a variation on the "How much?" question. But before you start discussing your fee, you need to make sure they're the right client for you. As they talk about themselves and their issues, ask yourself, "Is this a problem that can be resolved with hypnosis? As I engage with this person, how do I feel about them? What are their expectations about the process? Are they prepared to do the work necessary to be successful working with me?"

Remember, you're not selling potatoes. You're a serious professional providing a unique service. But they don't know that yet. They don't know what you can do. Or how you can help them. They're just thinking "*maybe* ... hypnosis can help." The problem is that we've all been socially conditioned to be savvy shoppers. It's just more comfortable to ask, "How much?" than it is to talk about the pain and the problem.

Three Essential Truths of Hypnosis

1. Not Everything Can Be Resolved with Hypnosis

Hypnosis is not a cure-all. There are limitations to what can be achieved with hypnosis. It's not magic. Is the problem the person is dealing with something that can reasonably be resolved using hypnosis?

You need to recognize that not *everything* can be resolved with hypnosis. You also need to know what *you're* capable of. After all, just because it's possible doesn't necessarily mean that *you* can do it. Are you *qualified* to work with the client's issue? Does it fit within your scope of practice? Do you have experience working with it? Know your limit and stay within it.

Some states have laws which limit what you can do in your practice. For example, you may be prohibited from physically touching your clients. Some states will throw you in jail if you use the word "therapist" without being a licensed professional. It's up to you to know which laws limit the scope of *your* practice.

2. Not Everyone is the Right Client for You.

How do you feel about this person? Do you like them? Do you want to work with them? Do you feel confident that you can help them with their issue? Are they a match for your level of knowledge and experience? These are important questions to answer before you schedule a person in for their first session. Bottom line - if you're *not* a match they won't benefit as much as they could, and you won't be as successful as you need to be to build your practice.

3. Not Everyone is Going to Be Ready

There is much you do to help prepare your clients to be successful working with you. But not everyone is going to be ready, willing, or able to do the work necessary to achieve the results they want. Some people have completely unrealistic expectations. For example, some people think they can just lie back and let you do all the work. Therapeutic hypnosis requires the client's participation. If the client is not willing to take an active role in their own healing, you're going to struggle to get results. They're not the right client for you!

If your prospective client meets the criteria of these three essential truths of hypnosis, continue the process of learning about their issue.

This is the beginning of the therapeutic relationship so help them to feel more comfortable with you. What you'll find is, the more you engage a person in conversation, the more invested they become in continuing the relationship with you. When that happens there will be a shift. They'll go from, "How much?" to "How soon can I get in?" That's when you book the first session. Feel excited! This could be the beginning of a beautiful relationship!

Summary:

Social gatherings are a great place to meet potential new clients but the place for an in-depth conversation about a person's issue is in the privacy of your office – either in person or over the phone. Don't make the mistake of standing off in the corner pouring over their problem.

Offering a free consultation is a way to invite more conversations free of any risk or obligation. The purpose of this call is to qualify your client. Don't make the mistake of turning it into a session.

Remember the three essential truths of hypnosis:

1. Not everything can be resolved with hypnosis.
2. Not everyone is the right client for you.
3. Not everyone is going to be ready to do the work required to be successful working with you.

CHAPTER 3:
Present Yourself

Marketing is about making sure that you are "top of mind." Top of mind means that when a person thinks "hamburger," they picture MacDonalds. When they think "coffee" they think "Starbucks." When a person thinks "hypnosis," or "stress relief," or "weight loss," or "emotional healing," or anything related to your business, you want them to think of *you*. The way to do this is to position yourself as the hypnosis expert. The easiest way I know to do that is something you're probably already doing. It's called education-based marketing.

Education Based Marketing is a very low-cost or no-cost way to promote your services and establish yourself as an authority in your field. If you educate your clients about hypnosis before your sessions, you already know how to do this. All you need to do is take your existing educational pre-talk, customize it to a specific problem, and use it to promote private sessions, self-hypnosis classes, or group programs.

Offering a free talk gives you access to free advertising opportunities you can use to create buzz about your business. For example, community newspaper stories, magazine listings, online event listings, social media posts, and press releases are ways to promote your practice and cost you nothing.

Think about all the problems you help people with. Create a list! Choose a specific problem that you're knowledgeable about and love to talk about. How could you educate people who are struggling with that issue? For example, hypnosis can help a person feel better about themselves. It can be used to improve relationships, enhance healing, manage pain, increase motivation, improve performance, and more.

Most people think of smoking and weight loss when they think of hypnosis, so this might be a good place to begin. This allows you to take advantage of an already established social perception that hypnosis is the answer. Or you could talk about something like having a healthy pregnancy, managing chronic pain, improving study skills, or finding your life purpose. The possibilities are endless.

What topics are you most knowledgeable about? What issues are you passionate about? What do you love to work with most? The trick is to pick a **specific** problem to center your talk around.

When you speak to a group, it's no different than speaking to one client with one problem. Just as you would in a private session, take your hypnosis pre-talk and make it relevant to that person's specific issue. You can mention other issues during your presentation. But the goal is to attract people who are struggling with a specific issue, then educate them about what you do and how you can help.

Who-What-How?

1. Who is your ideal client?
2. What specific issues do you most love to work with?
3. How can hypnosis make it easier to achieve a specific goal?
4. What are the common misconceptions about hypnosis?
5. What makes your approach different or unique?
6. How can you quickly give your audience a rewarding experience to prove that you just might be the answer they've been looking for?

Think of your group as *one person* who has that problem. Who is that "one person"? What specific problem are they struggling with? How can you help them get rid of that problem? Then share how hypnosis can make it easier for a person to get rid of the problem or achieve their goals.

What's their WIIFM? Talk about the benefits of change. Then, talk about "the hypnosis." It's not what most people think! Address the more common misconceptions about hypnosis. Answer questions. Talk about your approach. People who have never experienced hypnosis will be fascinated to learn what it's all about.

Once you have completed your pre-talk, teach your guests how to enter the state of hypnosis and it. Make it easy and give them a pleasant first experience of hypnosis. Then invite them to share what they experienced. Hypnosis is different for everybody, right?

One-Hour Presentation

I created a one-hour educational presentation on PowerPoint. I then followed the presentation with a 20-minute group hypnosis session. I highly recommend using PowerPoint for presentations and classes. It's relatively easy to learn and helps to keep the quality of presentations consistent. It's also an easy way to take control of your class time. If you're giving a talk at the Chamber of Commerce, you might only have 20 minutes. In this case, you won't have time to do a hypnosis session. But what you *can* do is give everyone a relaxation CD. That way, they can take you home with them!

Introductions

Begin your presentation by welcoming participants and thanking them for showing up. Then give a brief overview of what you're going to share. What are you going to talk about? Why should they pay attention to you? Who can benefit from learning from you? What are some of the benefits? Make it about *them* – not "the hypnosis".

Next, introduce yourself and offer a short list of your qualifications. Remember, the goal is to position yourself as "the expert". Some people are convinced by credentials. Briefly offer a few examples of conditions you have successfully worked with. If you're just starting out, offer a short list of issues that hypnosis can help to resolve or improve. (This is one place "menu marketing" can be useful!) For example:

- Self-confidence
- Self-esteem
- Anxieties, fears
- Relationship issues
- Weight loss
- Procrastination
- People-pleasing
- Depression
- Sleep problems
- Clarity & direction
- Stress management

- Cancer
- Childhood trauma
- Bereavement
- Money issues
- Goal achievement
- Troublesome dreams
- Blocks to creativity
- Emotional issues

Tell a Story

Do you have a story you can share that is relevant to your topic?[4] If so, keep it brief. A simple snapshot of the client before and after therapy can be a very effective marketing tool. For example, what symptoms did the client present with before the healing process? What else had they tried before coming to see you? What surprised them about the process? What was the "happy ending" to the client's story?

Teach How the Mind Works

Most people have no idea how the mind works. The language of the subconscious mind is image and emotion; use your PowerPoint presentation or a whiteboard to draw a picture. Show your group a simple mind model that illustrates the conscious and subconscious levels of the mind. Teach how these two parts of the mind operate differently. For example, the subconscious mind is responsible for all our habits and behaviors. It's responsible for all our feelings and emotions. It also controls body functions like salivation. (Imagine or think about a plump, juicy fresh lemon. See it, smell it, sense it, feel it. Now imagine that you are biting into that plump, juicy fresh lemon. Salivating?)

---

[4] Make sure you have written permission before sharing client stories.

Talk about stress; what it is, how it affects everyone, and how anything that is rooted in stress can be made better with hypnosis[5]. Talk about how we are programmed in childhood and how the Critical Faculty of the mind forms before the age of five or six years of age. Talk about the power of the subconscious mind and how feelings and emotions have the power to override reason and logic. (This is why diets don't work!) Then, explain *why* hypnosis can help; hypnosis gives us access to the internal thoughts, feelings, and beliefs which drive unwanted habits and behaviors, and generate unwanted symptoms.

Teach How Hypnosis Works

Hypnosis is not the new kid on the block. It's an ancient healing practice with a proven track-record for creating positive change. But many people don't know this. Tell them how hypnosis is a widely accepted adjunct therapy to healthcare, and how the power of suggestion is the basis of placebo in double-blind studies.

Be sure to address common misconceptions. Talk about the different kinds of hypnosis and how all hypnosis is self-hypnosis. Tell them *why* these are erroneous beliefs. For example, some people think hypnosis is sleep. Some people believe they can't be hypnotized. Some people think you're going to control them or make them bark like a chicken. (I like to add, "If you really *want* to bark like a chicken, I can help you with that!" This always gets a chuckle.)

---

[5] A great source of information about stress you can incorporate into presentations can be found in Alex Lloyd's book, The Healing Code.

Talk About How You Work

How is your approach different? What other services or programs do you offer? For example, I offered classes in self-hypnosis and dream work, as well as private one-on-one sessions.

Teach a Technique

Offer your participants "a gift" - something they can use right away to feel better. For example, I taught the EFT collarbone rubbing technique coupled with breathing for rapid stress relief. It only takes a few minutes, and most people notice a difference, right away. What's an easy technique you can teach in a few minutes?

Invitation to Experience Hypnosis

Wrap up your talk by thanking folks for giving you their time and attention. Then, invite those who would like to experience a short group hypnosis session to stay a little longer. Take a quick ten-minute potty break before coming back for a group hypnosis session to "de-stress and de-clutter the mind."

Conduct a Relaxation Hypnosis Session

When folks return for the group hypnosis session, set up before you begin the session. Get permission to guide them into hypnosis by letting them know what's going to happen. For example, "In a moment, I'm going to ask you to close your eyes. I'll give you some suggestions to help you to relax, a little. Then, I'm going to help you to release some of that internal stress and mental clutter you've been carrying around. Would that be okay?" I also like to set up a time-distortion test. This is an effective Convincer in a group setting provided you allow at least 20 minutes for the session to provide sufficient depth. To do a time distortion test, ask someone in the group to tell you what time it is. Ask them to remember the time for you. (Then make a note of it for your own reference.) This will ensure that, when you emerge the group from hypnosis, you'll have something to compare to.

Use relaxation hypnosis and give lots of deepening suggestions. Then, emerge with suggestions for positive expectancy. Immediately test the Convincer. Not everyone in the group will experience time distortion. That's okay. The ones who *do* experience time distortion will act as Convincers for those who didn't. Nice, right?

Signs of Hypnosis

Show the group a list of common signs of hypnosis. (I have a ready-made slide for this.)

- Heavy feeling
- Drifting or floating
- Sinking down feeling
- Warmth
- Tingling
- Twitching
- Swallowing
- Tears
- Time distortion

Point to your list and ask, "Who experienced any of these?"

These "signs of hypnosis" can act as Convincer while giving you another opportunity to remind the group that hypnosis is not what most people think! It's a very personal experience. It's different for everyone. For example, some people will experience sensations of heaviness or sinking down as they relax deeper into hypnosis. Others will feel lighter.

Warmth and tingling are commonly experienced because physical relaxation will allow an increase of blood circulation. Twitching is a sign that the nervous system of the body is releasing tension. Swallowing indicates relaxation of the throat muscles.

Awareness of any of these symptoms of hypnosis indicates some kind of change is occurring. That's good, right? Use it as proof that all hypnosis is self-hypnosis by saying, "You *did* that!" Let them own the power.

Post-Hypnosis Session Q & A

Invite participant questions. Validate their experience. Ask, "What did you learn tonight that you didn't know before?" Then give folks an opportunity to learn more about what they just experienced. End with an offer.

Make an Offer

Think about what your purpose is for giving a presentation. Then make them an offer they can't refuse. For example, you could offer a special rate on your next course, on a session package, a group program, or even their first private hypnosis session. Think about how you could combine group sessions with one-on-one sessions to help participants get better results!

How can they expect to benefit from your class or program? What aspects or issues require a more personal approach? How might your program prepare them for private sessions? How will it save them money? **For example, if** you want to use your presentation to get more private session clients, remind folks that deeply rooted emotional issues require a more personal touch. Then give some examples of the many issues that can benefit more from private sessions.

If you want to use your presentation to get people to sign up for your self-hypnosis course, remind them that there is much a person can do for themselves. Give examples of how self-hypnosis can be effective in dealing with specific issues such as reducing stress or improving sleep (both major contributors to weight problems!)

The idea is to offer an incentive for making the decision *now* and not later. You want them to act now! Just make sure they have reasonable expectations. Promising the moon won't get you more clients if you can't deliver. Remember, hypnosis isn't magic. (But it sure can seem that way, sometimes.)

Give a Reward

At the end of your presentation, have something extra you can give your guests as a special thank you for sharing their time with you. It doesn't have to cost you much. It could be a free audio recording, or a tip list related to the topic of the presentation. Alternatively, you could have a draw for a gift certificate or gift basket. I used to give out coupons worth $25 toward their *first session*. (These had expiry dates of thirty days.)

Regardless of whether they choose to take advantage of your special offer, give them a gift with no strings attached. Think about how you can use this to stay "top of mind" with them. For example, you could pre-record the relaxation session they just enjoyed with you. This means they get to take you home with them. This is something that can bring business to you for years to come because it will be passed on to friends and family members. I used to give every new client a relaxation CD to take home after their first session. This allowed them to enjoy the benefits of relaxing into hypnosis with me, again. Many reported that it helped them to sleep better.

Make sure everything you hand out to clients has your contact information on it. Treat it like a business card. Remember, anything you put out there can double as marketing for your services. Information you share could get passed along to others. Make it easy for people to contact you if they like what they see/hear.

Smile!

Put your friendly face on all your promotional material including your website, business card, brochures, posters, etc. Remember, a picture is worth a thousand words, and you don't get a second chance at a first impression. Go pro. Don't make the mistake of using that great photo of you at the family barbeque! Invest in a professional headshot.

To promote my free introductory talk, I created a postcard[6] with all the key information. I uploaded my photo and put it on the front of the card. On the back, I put the relevant information. i.e., Who is this for? What is it about? How will they benefit from attending? What action do they need to take? At the bottom, I left a blank area where I could fill in the date of the next talk. I then distributed these cards at every opportunity. For example, if I went to a coffee shop, I'd leave one on the table. Whenever I attended a social event, I'd make sure to have some in my bag.

Summary:

Education-based marketing is a way for you to position yourself as the hypnosis expert. You want to be "top of mind" so that, when a person thinks "hypnosis," or "stress relief," or "weight loss," or "emotional healing," or anything related to your business, they think of *you*.

---

[6] Vistaprint.com. A postcard is like an oversized business card.

Remember to put your photo on your marketing material. Your goal is to position yourself at the top of mind

Create a list of problems that you can help people with. Be specific. Then take your educational pre-talk and customize it to that specific issue. Remember, speaking to a group is no different than speaking to a client in a private session.

One-Hour Presentation

1. Introductions
2. Tell a story
3. Teach how the mind works
4. Teach how hypnosis works
5. Talk about how you work
6. Teach a simple technique
7. Invite participants to experience hypnosis
8. Conduct a relaxation hypnosis session
9. Emerge with convincers
10. Answer questions
11. Make an offer
12. Give a reward

CHAPTER 4:
Teach Self-Hypnosis Classes

Sheila is a gifted healer who combines bodywork with counseling and hypnosis. She has a body-mind approach to healing that is highly effective and gets great results. She loves what she does. Sheila's degree in Social Work has given her the ability to work both within and outside of the healthcare system. Unfortunately, this entails a tremendous amount of paperwork. When Sheila realized that she was waiting up to six months to get paid for state-funded clients, she decided to bust loose from the bureaucracy.

Sheila had long-ago realized that clients who pay for their own therapy get better quicker than their insurance-funded counterparts. Rather than turn down paying work, she had continued, albeit begrudgingly, to fill out the required forms. But the thought of liberating herself from the burden of all the paperwork made her heart sing. She rejoiced at the thought of finally being free to focus on what mattered most – healing work.

Unfortunately, Sheila did not have a strategy for bringing in more paying clients to replace the ones she would be turning away. Before long she was feeling the crunch financially. That's when Sheila decided to draw upon another one of her gifts – teaching.

Sheila started to hold classes in the reception area of her clinic. Not only did this limit her class sizes to fit within the confines of the waiting room, but it also failed to bring in new clients. Sheila was drawing students from her existing client-base. As a result, she was restricting the amount of income derived from each class. It didn't take long for her to run out of paying students.

I learned something important from Sheila. When it comes to self-promotion, healing practitioners tend to do things backwards. Marketing takes a back seat while we focus on what matters most - helping our clients to heal. As a result, the inflow of new clients is sporadic, at best. Instead of following Sheila's strategy, I started using self-hypnosis classes to market myself and my services. Instead of trying to upsell my clients to my classes, I funneled students out of the classroom and into my chair. What I discovered is that teaching self-hypnosis classes is a great way to build your reputation as a hypnosis professional while doing something you love. It's also a great way to get more clients into your hypnosis chair, which will help you to grow your business.

The way to funnel clients into private sessions is to use your self-hypnosis class to *empower* your participants. Show them the power of their own mind. Let them surprise themselves! Then educate them about all the various issues they can resolve *on their own*. You can use the same educational pre-talk you would use in your one-on-one sessions. Just make delivering it an interactive process so that you can adapt to the needs of each individual student. Invite lots of questions. Get them engaged and make the information relevant to each person. Then show them how just a few minutes in hypnosis can help them to feel better.

Your students will become ambassadors for your services once *they know* that hypnosis is a safe and effective solution to resolving a variety of problems. Having experienced hypnosis, they'll *know* how much better it can help them to feel. When they learn self-hypnosis, they'll feel empowered. They'll *know* that hypnosis works and will want to share you with others. It's like Ghost Busters. Who ya gonna call? YOU, your friendly neighborhood hypnotherapist. That's who! Show that you can be trusted, show that you care, and demonstrate how you can help. Then watch the referrals come your way.

Results Will Get You Referrals

A strong and successful hypnosis practice is built upon the success stories of your clients. Teaching self-hypnosis classes will generate more clients for you. Especially if you put your students' success first. Build your reputation for offering a superior service and you'll grow a referral-based business. Then you won't have to spend every waking moment worrying about getting the next client.

People who attended my classes got to know me. Once they got to know me, they trusted me. As a result, many would go on to book private sessions. They also referred their friends and family members to me. I found that about 40% of my 7th Path Self-Hypnosis™ students signed up for private sessions, either during or after completing the class. Many sent me their spouse, children, friends, or co-workers to attend my classes or for private sessions.

What I had discovered was an organic way to get new clients into my office and into the chair. Not only that. Sheila's costly mistakes had taught me a fun way to add an extra $10,000 to my income!

It took some trial-and-error to figure out the most effective approach. But in the end, I found a sweet spot! For example, I tried offering a five-part course, but it was too much of a time-commitment for most people. I tried chunking down to a three-part course, but I kept bumping into scheduling problems. I even tried a one-day class, which resolved the scheduling issue. The problem was that it didn't allow me to make sure the students were doing the practice correctly. I wanted my students to be successful because results will get you referrals.

When you show them how they can achieve the results they want, they'll happily send you referrals. Every one of your students knows someone else you can help. It might be their sister who is struggling to quit smoking, or their best friend who suffers from panic attacks, or a child struggling in school. You have just trained an army of ambassadors who *know* that you can help!

> **Marketing Tip:**
> *Create a feedback form for your students to fill out before completing the class. This is testimonial gold!*

The Sweet Spot

In the end, the solution was a two-day course offered over two Saturdays (or Sundays.) This was the sweet spot - doable for most people while giving me a way to check on students' progress. The first class included a comprehensive educational pre-talk followed by a group hypnosis session.

Once everyone had experienced hypnosis, I taught them how to take themselves into hypnosis and emerge themselves. Students would then have a week to practice at home on their own. When they returned for the second class, I could check on their progress, answer questions (there were lots!), and make sure that everyone was doing the practice correctly. After addressing questions and problems, I could then deepen the student's experience of self-hypnosis by facilitating multiple group hypnosis sessions.

An Affordable Option

Self-hypnosis is a self-empowerment tool that allows a person to do their own work of healing. There is much that a person can do for themselves. *If only they knew how!* You can teach them how! Not only is a self-hypnosis class a very profitable client-attractor for your healing practice, but it also gives you an affordable option you can offer. For example, if someone is on the fence about committing to private sessions, you can offer your self-hypnosis class as an alternative to private, one-on-one sessions.

Having a self-hypnosis course to offer also gives you a lower-cost option for folks who think they "can't afford" your session fee. For most people, "I can't afford" is nothing more than social programming that has them stuck in 'scarcity thinking.' Sure, in some cases it may be true. They may be temporarily working with limited resources. Regardless, you can still help them to help themselves. After all, all hypnosis is essentially self-hypnosis! You can teach them how! And when you offer a prospective client a choice of how to proceed, they're going to choose *you*.

Convert to Private Sessions

When a person learns self-hypnosis from you in a class they get to know you in a safe environment. The group provides safety. Educating a person about the power of their mind is empowering them. When you show that you care enough to empower them, they're going to consider you a trusted friend. This establishes a powerful rapport! You're teaching them how to create positive change for themselves by giving them a tool they can use for the rest of their lives. This dispels the idea that you have all the power while establishing you as an expert!

Guiding a person through hypnosis multiple times proves to them that hypnosis is safe. It gives them the time they need to relax and experience some depth. It also conditions them to the sound of your voice. As a result, they'll find it very easy to go into hypnosis working with you privately. Think of your class as a way of preparing future clients for the work you will do with them in private sessions.

Recognize that some of your students are going to have deeper issues that require more help. Be sure to include this in your pre-talk. Once you have taught them the kinds of issues that respond well to self-hypnosis, teach them what sorts of issues are considered "deeper issues" that generally require more help. Let them put two and two together on their own.

Assure your students that their self-hypnosis practice will allow them to take care of the "ordinary, everyday stresses of daily living." They don't need you for that. They can take care of it on their own. But sometimes there are deeper issues they might need help in resolving. For example, "One of the things that can happen when you start doing your own work, is that your subconscious mind starts pushing "stuff" to the surface. That's good! We want that stuff out! You don't need it. When that happens, realize your subconscious mind wants this stuff resolved. *If you find yourself bumping into something that seems a bit much, or you start feeling stuck in your practice, the solution is simple. Pick up the phone and call me. Book a private session and we'll take care of it.* Because you have this practice under your belt, the healing work we do together will be much quicker and easier, which will save you money."

At the end of your self-hypnosis course, remind your students that they now have a powerful tool to help them feel better – *if they use it*. Encourage them to keep up their daily practice. Then, remind them that some issues can require additional help. Let them know that, should they bump into something that they need help with, you're here to help. Then offer a special rate on an "upgrade" to private sessions.

Offering an incentive costs you nothing because you're getting a client who has already been through your pre-talk. It's like getting paid to promote one-on-one sessions while, at the same time, pre-qualifying your clients. You'll have established rapport with them and reduced resistance to the process. You'll have already conditioned them for hypnosis and they will have shown, through daily practice, that they are willing to do their own work of self-healing. This gives you a qualified client who is ready to go to work!

Even if they don't become your client right away, they will remember you. They may call you up in a few weeks or months when they're ready to get started working on their issue.

Self-hypnosis students will be some of your best hypnosis clients ever! They are already active participants in their own healing and have a practice they can use between sessions to accelerate the healing process. Most people are very surprised with how much more powerful a private session is compared to a group session. And because you have already educated them to have reasonable expectations about the process, most will be prepared to invest in a multi-session program. All of which will get you better results.

Get Paid More

Back in 2010, I charged $250 for my two-day 7th Path Self-Hypnosis™ course and $100 for a six-hour dream working class[7]. On average, I got paid about $1,500 a day for having fun. That's not factoring in all the clients that signed up for private sessions.

The self-hypnosis course included a practitioner's workbook, a practice CD (with a recording of my voice), plus a bonus book[8].

Upon completion, each student received an attractive certificate. The materials cost me about $25 per person. You don't need a large class. Nor does it take many classes to earn an extra $10,000 in income.

- 5 students = $1,250 - $125 material cost = $1,125 net
- 10 students = $2,500 - $250 material cost = $2,250 net
- 15 students = $3,750 - $375 material cost = $ 3,375 net

The Value is Obvious

I hope you can appreciate how this makes a self-hypnosis class an affordable option for a lot of people who might otherwise walk away. You're offering them a way to gain from your expertise without having

---

[7] Now available as a book, Dream Healing Practitioner Guidebook: *A Healer's Guide to Uncovering the Secret Messages of Your Dreams.*

[8] The Secret Language of Feelings by Calvin Banyan.

to fork out a big upfront expense. They can have fun learning a new skill that can truly help them. And they can do it with their friends! My 7th Path Self-Hypnosis™ program included six group hypnosis sessions – two sessions in the first class, four sessions in the second class. This made it easy to sell the program because, if you were to pay me for six private sessions, it would cost you $1,500.

The value is obvious. The person is getting $1,500 worth of hypnosis for $250. Plus, they're learning how to do it themselves. You might be thinking, "But if I teach self-hypnosis classes, they won't come to me for private sessions." Nuh-uh! Nothing could be farther from the truth. In fact, I encourage prospective clients to attend my self-hypnosis training *before* beginning private sessions with me. Why? Simple. I'm lazy. : -) I don't want to have to work any harder than necessary.

A class gives me the luxury of time to deliver a much more substantial pre-talk than I ever could in my office. This saves me time during the first session! For the price of a single session, they're receiving a seriously powerful learning experience that conditions them for hypnotherapy, should they wish to "graduate" into private sessions.

The educational pre-talk[9] lays the foundation for success - yours and the clients. When you guide a person in and out of hypnosis repeatedly, it compounds the state, allowing the student to experience deeper states very quickly. Having the experience of deeper states gives students the opportunity to realize they really are experiencing hypnosis. That's important because the worst enemy of hypnosis

---

[9] Radical Healing: Hypnosis Practitioner's Guide to Harnessing the Healing Power of the Educational Pre-Talk

practitioners everywhere is negative press. I've heard it and so have you. "I don't think I was hypnotized." "It worked for a while but then …" "I tried it, and it didn't work." You can guide your students to first *realize* that hypnosis is really happening, and then to *feel proud* for having accomplished it.

Group validation also helps to solidify everyone's experience of this. Reinforce this new level of learning because, now that they know it's true, that all hypnosis is *self*-hypnosis, it removes *the fear* of hypnosis.

The more time you get to spend with a person, the more rapport you're going to have, which will get you better results. The more a person does hypnosis with you, the more conditioned they are to follow your instructions. As a result, they will tend to be more compliant when they finally come in for their first private session with you. This makes your job easier. If they do even a little self-hypnosis practice before coming in for a personal session, your client will be virtually push-button, which means that you'll be able to dive into the deeper work that much sooner. In other words, it saves you time, and gets them deeper, which results in healing quicker.

Self-Hypnosis Class Outline

Th following is an outline for my 7th Path Self-Hypnosis™ course. The first four parts are delivered on Day One. Students then had a week to practice on their own. What you will find is that, once students have mastered taking themselves into hypnosis and emerging themselves, subsequent sessions will take them deeper into the state.

Ditch the Pitch!

Day One:

Part 1: Introductions

- Participant introductions
- Introduce topic
- Introduce yourself

Part 2: Educational Pre-Talk

- How does the mind work?
- How does hypnosis work?
- What will I experience in hypnosis? (Most common experiences)
- Any questions?

Part 3: Group Hypnosis Session

- Set up for Convincer
- Guided group-hypnosis session with lots of deepening
- Emerge and test Convincer
- Group share, answer questions

Part 4: How to Take Yourself into Hypnosis

- Preliminary instructions on how to practice self-hypnosis
- Hypnosis session to install trigger to re-induce hypnosis.[10]

---

[10] 7th Path™ uses a key phrase to re-induce hypnosis. Gerald Kein uses a light switch image and finger tap. Jaimie Feldman uses the person's favorite color and single-digit number as a re-induction cue. Parkhill forms the "O" by placing the thumb and

- Emerge and immediately have participants re-induce hypnosis using trigger
- Deepening suggestions
- Post-hypnotic suggestions to compound trigger
- Emerge, group share
- Answer questions

Part 5: Reinforce the Trigger

- Repeat re-induction practice
- Offer deepening suggestions
- Give instructions on how to self-emerge. For example, count from one to five and open eyes.
- Emerge, group share
- Answer questions

Once you have installed the trigger, you don't need to do an induction. Just have your students close their eyes and take themselves into hypnosis using their trigger.

Allow a few moments for them to enter the state, then offer suggestions to deepen the state. If you like, you can then continue with a short script of your choice. For example, you could reinforce the benefits of practicing self-hypnosis daily, enjoying the benefits of

---

forefinger together. Silva Mind Control Method uses a blackboard to count back while erasing numbers.

having a regular self-hypnosis practice, increasing well-being, improved sleep, and so on. Allow a few minutes of silence to simply enjoy the state. Then, emerge the class by giving the suggestion to use their emerging count to emerge themselves. Easy-peezy.

Day Two:

On day two of my 7th Path Self-Hypnosis™ course, students were guided in and out of hypnosis multiple times. In between each hypnosis session, I taught them how to give themselves hypnotic suggestions, answered their questions, and generally reinforced all the learning.

Part 6: How to Give Yourself Hypnotic Suggestions

- What is a suggestion?
- Rules for formulating effective suggestions
- Use of imagery and emotion
- Practice session(s) using a specific suggestion.

Make success easy!

If you're teaching a self-hypnosis class, think about how you can make it easier for participants to be successful. Remember, making it easy for your students to be successful will generate referrals which will help to grow your practice. If they do the practice they'll get the results. One of the things you can do to make it easier to keep up their practice is to provide students with printed instructions on how to practice self-hypnosis and formulate suggestions. Remember to make sure everything you hand out has your contact information on it. Make it easy for people to contact you if they have further questions or want to book a private session with you.

When you teach self-hypnosis, students experience the state of hypnosis multiple times with you. This anchors the state to the sound of your voice. When a person listens to you, again and again, they become conditioned to the sound of your voice. This can make it much easier for them to trust you in private sessions. If you provide an audio recording of deepening suggestions[11] your students can take you home with them! Having a recording of your voice counting them down to a deeper level of awareness can be a big help for a lot of people. Your students will love how easily they can enjoy deeper states of hypnosis. This can help to keep them motivated to stick with their practice long enough for it to become a habit.

Deepening CD

Begin with instructions: *Do not use this recording while driving or operating heavy machinery.* Then instruct the listener to get into a comfortable position where they won't be disturbed for the next few moments. Follow this with the suggestion, "In a moment . . ." Then tell them what's going to happen. For example, you could choose to use a soft tone or a chime to signal the beginning of the practice period. In this case, say, "In a moment you will hear a tone. At the sound of the tone, take yourself into hypnosis using your trigger."

Alternately, you could simply say, "Begin Now." Then, leave an interval of approximately *20 seconds of silence* at the beginning. This will give the student time to take themselves into hypnosis.

---

[11] You can easily create your own CDs with Audacity. Royalty Free music can be purchased online. Harry Henshaw offers a selection of low-cost music tracks. Also, the National Guild of Hypnotists has a couple of Royalty Free music CDs.

When the period of silence ends, begin speaking softly and quietly. Deliver about 20 minutes of deepening suggestions. You can use progressive muscle relaxation as a deepener. You can use a series of deepening counts. You can use imagery such as steps going down to a deeper level. Or any combination you like. My preference is to simply use a deepening count. For example: (following the 20 seconds of silence, speak softly) *Gently now ... as you continue listening to the sound of MY voice, allow yourself to go deeper with each and every gentle breath that you exhale ...*

In a moment ... I'm going to count from 10 down to 1 ... I'm going to count down THREE TIMES ... And each time you hear the number ONE ... DOUBLE the relaxation. Each time you hear the number ONE ... let yourself go twice as deep... Each time you hear the number ONE you will be many, many, MANY times deeper ... Each time you hear the number ONE you will be deeper than the time before. ... Let's begin.... 10 ... 9, deeper now. Deeper relaxed. Doubling the relaxation as you continue to go deeper, deeper, down.

For the first two counts of 10 down to 1, deliver intermittent suggestions. For the final count, just do the count with an increasingly long pause after each count. When you reach the count of ONE just whisper it.

10 ... 9 .... 8 ..... 7 ...... 6 .... 5 .... 4 .... 3 .... 2 ...... (whisper) ONE.

Then after you whisper the count of "ONE" ... allow a 10 second period of silence before giving an emerging count.

During the emerging count, include suggestions for the benefits of repeat practice. For example: *Each time you enter into a state of hypnosis you will go deeper. And the deeper you go, the better you feel. And the better you feel, the deeper you CAN go. This brings you all the wonderful benefits of change. And all the rewards, because YOU REALIZE ... change is a GOOD thing for you now.*

Stay in Touch

To stay in touch, I created a series of five weekly newsletters corresponding with each of the classes. Once created, I had a ready-made email series ready to mail out. All I had to do was change the dates for upcoming events. The first newsletter welcomed new students to 'the Path.'

Each subsequent newsletter acted as a refresher for each lesson and a reminder to the students to keep up their practice. This meant that for five weeks following the class I was showing up in the students' email box to encourage them to keep up their practice. They loved it. I know this because I got plenty of emails in response. Some said "Thanks." Others emailed to ask questions. Know that when people reply to your emails, it shows that what you're doing is working. You're connecting with people. They're glad to hear from you. They consider you a friend in need.

Make sure each newsletter you send out has your picture and contact information on it. Think of your emails as a continuation of your educational pretalk. For example, my emails included:

- A motivational quote that was relevant to each lesson.
- A short article relating to self-hypnosis.
- Reminders of how and when to do self-hypnosis practice.
- Tips for improving your self-hypnosis practice.
- Updates on future class offerings.

Facilitate Groups

Offering group programs is a great way to promote your services and gives you a way to make your services more available to more people by making them more affordable. Group programs are especially ideal for smoking and weight loss because they offer the added benefit of multiple sessions coupled with peer support. Plus, your per-hour fee is much higher in a class or group setting.

Group sessions have been shown to be very effective when used as part of a healing program. The group itself provides the benefits of peer support and accountability and helps people stay committed to their program. An ongoing group can be very effective when used in conjunction with personal session work. You can teach basic concepts and techniques in the group which will then save time in private sessions. This reduces the cost to the client while giving you clients who are ready to do the deeper work.

Using the group setting to teach general concepts and self-healing techniques will save time in private sessions. For example, you can present your educational pre-talk and teach how the mind works, how hypnosis works, and how healing happens. Self-healing strategies like self-hypnosis, tapping, and breathing techniques are easy to teach in a group setting and can be used to empower participants in the group. They can then use these techniques on their own to support their success.

A group program can function the same way a self-hypnosis class does by setting your students up for one-on-one sessions. This sets *you* up to be more successful because the clients coming in for private sessions are already primed to be successful working with you. You'll have an established rapport, they'll understand the process, they'll have reasonable expectations, and they'll be ready to dive into deeper work. As a result, you'll feel much more confident guiding the process. All of which makes your job easier.

Summary:

Teaching self-hypnosis classes is an effective way to build your reputation as a hypnosis expert. Not only is it fun, but it's a way also to get paid more. You don't need a large class to add $10,000 to your income.

A self-hypnosis class can be an affordable option you can offer to people who are on the fence with regards to private sessions. When you have an option you can offer, they're more likely to choose you!

Your self-hypnosis class can attract more clients for private sessions. Once a person has learned self-hypnosis, they may be converted to private sessions if they have deeper issues they wish to work on. Because they have shown a willingness to do their own work of self-healing, they're qualified to be your client! Think of your class as priming your ideal client for their first session by establishing rapport, providing proof, and giving you more time to deliver a comprehensive pre-talk.

During the class, your students will experience the state of hypnosis multiple times with you, anchoring the state to the sound of your voice. Providing an audio recording to support practice at home can help to increase your student's success practicing self-hypnosis. A two-day class is more doable for most people and allows you to test the results between sessions. Ensuring your self-hypnosis students are successful will get you referrals.

Day One:

1. Introductions
2. Educational Pre-talk
3. Group hypnosis session
4. Self-induction process
5. Reinforce the self-induction trigger

Day Two:

6. How to give yourself hypnotic suggestions

Stay in touch with your students by creating an email series. Once you have drafted a template, all you need to do is change the dates.

Think about how you can customize your self-hypnosis class for specific issues. Group facilitation can give you another way to make your services available to more people by making them more affordable. Additionally, group programs can be personalized by combining personal one-on-one sessions with group sessions.

The purpose of your client attraction system is not to sell a person anything. It's to get the attention of your ideal client and get them to call you.

CHAPTER 5:
Get Organized

Giving presentations and teaching self-hypnosis classes is an effective business strategy that requires an investment of time and money. To get the best results, be prepared to invest in tools and equipment that will support you in offering a high-quality learning experience for your students. Ideally, you want to choose equipment that will save you time, make you more efficient, and ensure that you're consistently teaching the same material from one class to another.

Use PowerPoint.

In my opinion PowerPoint is the way to go. Build it once and your course becomes plug and play! It doesn't get any easier than this. You can revise your presentation anytime to tweak or upgrade your material, as needed. Plus, it helps to keep you on time and on topic while ensuring you are teaching the same material consistently from one class to the next.

When you're delivering a paid program, you want to cover all the information you've promised. The worst thing you can do is to start taking short cuts and skipping over important information! PowerPoint will help you to consistently deliver the same course material, over and over again. This ensures that all your students get the same value from your program.

You also need to respect people's time and wrap your program within a certain time frame. With PowerPoint you can allot a certain amount of time to each segment. This will help you to know where you need to be in your presentation to be able to wrap up on time. Overall, PowerPoint makes time-management easier. That's a lot of bang for your investment buck!

What equipment do you need?

To use PowerPoint in a class setting you're going to need a computer, projector and projection screen. I keep all my PowerPoint presentations on a dedicated notebook computer. It's small and light and only cost a few hundred dollars. I purchased a Benq projector (cost about $400) and a used roll-up projection screen (cost $50). You may be able to plug your computer into a big screen TV, if there's one available. If so, you'll have to check to see if it will work with your laptop. Any hotel that hosts conferences will have a built-in presentation system which they will rent you for a fee. But don't assume. Verify that this is an option before showing up to teach your class.

I have a portable classroom that fits in the back of my car. It's very compact and provides everything I need to teach a class anywhere. My classroom system is comprised of a notebook computer, projector, portable projector screen, whiteboard, dry-erase markers, CD player, several extension cords, a roll of shipping tape, and a couple of boxes of tissues. Apart from the projector screen, everything fits into a large Rubbermaid bin.

Make it Engaging

In a group setting you want participants to pay attention to what you have to say. The way to accomplish this is to get them engaged with you while you're delivering your course material. If you don't choose to use PowerPoint, use something visual like a whiteboard or a flip chart. This helps to inject some action into your presentation while giving you a way to emphasize key points. Remember to write big to ensure the people in the back row can see it. Use several different colored markers to add impact to your message. Think about how you can make your presentation more interesting and engaging.

Keep it Simple

The biggest mistake most people make with PowerPoint is trying to put an entire script on one screen. Whatever you use, don't fill the screen or whiteboard with gobs of text. This tends to either bore or overwhelm people. Bullet points are all that's needed[12]. Use a maximum of three or four bullet items on each slide. Keep your presentation simple.

Use Imagery

Image and emotion are the languages of the subconscious mind. Visual types learn better when there are images, and most people will pay

---

[12] Cheater Tip: If you're using a flipchart, you may need something to refer to while you're delivering your content. Before your class, lightly pencil in your bullet point! This will help to keep you on track and on time.

attention if you can add some entertainment value to your presentation. Images can help you make your presentation more interesting and entertaining.

The last thing you want to do is start reading streams of text off your presentation slides. It's boring and it looks like you don't know the material. Use images. Draw pictures, diagrams, models. Invite participants to ask questions as you move through the key points. Make it interesting. **Remember, this is a digital format.** This means you have an unlimited supply of slides.

Less is more when it comes to an individual slide. But more is better when it comes to the number of slides you use. The more slides you create, the less time you'll spend on each slide as you teach your class. This will help to keep things moving along, which will help to hold people's attention to what you have to say. It will also help you to stay on topic and end on time.

Keep Notes Handy

PowerPoint provides an area for notes which you can reference during your presentation. I'm a bit of a technophobe and I don't like to do things off-the-cuff, so when I first started teaching classes, I printed out my presentation notes. I slid them into plastic protectors and placed them into a binder for easy reference. This gave me something to reference while I was guiding the class through the slide presentation.

When I bought a tablet, I transferred all my notes onto it. To set up your presentation notes on a tablet, print your PowerPoint presentation to a pdf file. Then transfer them into whatever app you have chosen for your device.

Ditch the Pitch!

The advantage of using a tablet is that it's backlit, which allows you to see your notes in a low-light situation. Plus, it's compact. You can slip it into your handbag or satchel and you're good to go. A tablet is also much lighter than a binder. This makes it the perfect solution for air-travel. Some people prefer to use their mobile phone. That's okay, too, but I prefer the larger screen of a tablet. Plus, you don't run the risk of getting a call in the middle of your class. Awkward!

You can buy an adapter that will allow you to mount your tablet on a camera stand. This gives you a portable podium allowing you to teach classes hands-free. Suh-weet!

Structure Your Class Time

It's important to respect your student's time. People have lives they want to get back to. Structuring your class will help you to start on time and end on time. This will allow you to leave your students feeling great about having spent their valuable time with you.

Start by creating a basic outline[13]. Then, estimate how much time you will need to cover the material. For example, for a one-hour presentation you need to allow 20 minutes for the hypnosis session and 10 minutes for debriefing. That leaves 30 minutes for your introduction and educational pre-talk. A 90-minute talk will give you a full hour to deliver your material before guiding the group through hypnosis.

---

[13] If you create a generic template, you can use it to create any number of informational talks, classes, or programs. Just adapt it to the specific topic and you're good to go!

Allow plenty of short breaks.

Frequent breaks will make it easier for you to hold people's attention. People start to lose the ability to absorb information about every 45 minutes to an hour. Bladders get full. Depending on the length of your presentation or class, make appropriate time allowances for potty breaks, grab a beverage, have a snack, or just get up and move around.

Allow extra time for the lunch break.

When you're teaching a full-day class, you need to allow extra time for people to travel to and from a lunch spot. Sometimes there are lineups which can mean delays. When people are pressed for time that just adds stress. You're trying to help them de-stress!

If the class is going out for lunch, you'll need to allow additional time for getting there and waiting for a table. Usually, 90 minutes for lunch is reasonable. Consider breaking early (11:30) or later (1:00) to avoid the lunch-hour rush.

When people go out for lunch there are always going to be stragglers. They get talking with a classmate, lose track of time, and will scurry in late with apologies. This disrupts your schedule. If you're planning on going straight into a hypnosis session after lunch, this will hold up the whole class. Is there a lunch-spot within easy walking distance of the class? If not, consider inviting people to bring a bagged lunch. A 60-minute lunch break is ample time if everyone eats in. Bring along a few extra food items. There's always someone who forgets their lunch!

Keep it Relevant

While you talk about how the mind works, how hypnosis works, and how you help people make your presentation relevant to your topic. For example, you can talk about how problems like smoking or overeating are learned behaviors. Often these problems started as ways of coping with stressors early in life. Because *the behavior worked* it got repeated. Over time it became a habit. But it's not the real problem. The problem is the internal drive to smoke that is being generated by the subconscious mind. Smoking is a subconscious solution to a deeper problem.

The same is true of weight problems. The weight isn't the problem, it's what's driving the person to overeat. Eating is a subconscious solution. This sets you up to talk about how resolving the internal drive can get rid of the problem – for good!

Talk about stress. Everybody's got stress to deal with. Time stress. Money stress. Relationship stress. Too much information. Too little time. Then you can talk about how hypnosis can help to relieve the ordinary stress of everyday living. This sets you up to guide them through a short relaxation (stressbusting) hypnosis session.

Remember, if you take a brief potty break before beginning the hypnosis session, it will make it easier for people to relax during the session. People who are antsy, or not interested, can take advantage of the break to leave before you start the hypnosis session.

Make it Interactive

Allowing people to interact with you while you teach them about the process will help to keep people engaged. It also helps to increase rapport with you. If you're working with a smaller group (less than ten people) this is an effective way to encourage group bonding.

If you have a larger group, you may find it less disruptive to plan for short Q&A periods, instead. In this case, ask the group to hold off on their questions until you ask for them. Invite them to write their questions down so that they'll remember. Then chunk things down. Teach a short segment, then invite questions before moving onto the next chunk. To encourage questions, ask your participants questions based on what you have just taught them. This will help them to feel smart!

The more you can get people participating, the more engaged people will be. It's easier to learn anything when it's fun. So, make it fun. And keep things moving along quickly.

Provide Handouts

Having a worksheet or an outline that you can give to participants as a handout can make your talk more interactive. If you're giving a short presentation, a follow along/fill-in-the-blanks handout can help keep participants more engaged. Kinesthetic types learn better by doing something physically. If you give them something to DO, you'll hold their attention longer.

When facilitating a program, a workbook that outlines all the steps, has diagrams, definitions, etc. gives your students something they can refer to later. Handouts save them from having to take a lot of notes. It's encouraging to see people taking notes. This tells you that they're finding good value in what you have to say. But you want them to pay attention to *you*. You want them to engage with *you*, not be scribbling furiously to capture all the vital information you're sharing. If you use a written exercise, make sure that it helps your participants to feel smart. Don't make it an exam. Make it about helping folks to feel good about themselves. They'll associate those good feelings with you.

Use Relaxation Hypnosis

In hypnosis school, most of us learned how to facilitate relaxation hypnosis *first* because it's slow and gentle. When you're learning, you need to slow things down. This allows you to observe a person's responses to your suggestions, which helps to develop your observation skill in sessions. In a therapeutic setting, rapid inductions are a better use of your time simply because a rapid induction only takes a few minutes, leaving the rest of your session to focus on the client's problem and helping them achieve their results. That's what they're paying for.

In a group session, you don't have the ability to monitor individual responses. You need a more general approach that will be effective for most people. Relaxation hypnosis gives you this. Because most people don't have any resistance to learning how to relax, the process of "relaxing into hypnosis" can seem less threatening.

I prefer the Elman Induction for group sessions. I then add progressive relaxation as a deepening technique. This works very well. I like the Elman Induction because it's a formal induction procedure. The instructions are very step-by-step. And it's very clear when the hypnosis begins. For the same reason, I use a formal count-up to emerge the group. This makes it clear to participants when the hypnosis session is beginning and when it is ending.

Have a Clear Beginning and Ending

In the Elman Induction the first step is to close the eyes. You can formalize this step by making it into a series of concrete steps. Here's how I do it.

1. Take a deep breath in, fill up the lungs …
2. Hold it, hold it, hold it …
3. And now exhale, relax, and close the eyes.

This is a more formal approach than just "close your eyes and relax." It has three steps. This establishes a clear beginning to the induction process while allowing you to see whether the group is following instructions. You can use these same three steps to start the induction in your one-on-one sessions.

In a private session, eye-closure is a test for compliance. "Compliance" means cooperation. It has nothing to do with control. You're just testing to confirm that the client is following your instructions. For example, if the client closes their eyes before you tell them to, they're jumping at the gun. That means they're not following instructions, which means you're not in charge of the session. It happens.

When it happens, I use a little humor and say, "Wait! Don't start without me!" I then start the process over. This establishes, right out of the gate, who's in charge of the session. (It had better be you!) A "do-over" can be very effective for nipping a problem in the bud!

In a group session, you picture your group as an orchestra. You're the conductor. When you tell them to hold the breath for a few seconds, you should see a little tension present because holding the breath builds up a little pressure inside. Then, when they exhale, it releases that little bit of pressure. There's a natural relaxation response that goes with this. The sensation that goes with the exhale is a kind of a sinking *down* sensation. This is a good time to add the suggestion, "and go deeper" because it's congruent with the person's experience. The suggestion will feel true.

Make Participants Responsible

Whether you're delivering an introductory presentation, a hypnosis pre-talk, or teaching a class, be very clear on one point - all hypnosis is self-hypnosis. You can't *make* a person change. *You* don't have the power. The *power* exists in the person's own mind. What *you* can do is teach them how to gain access to that power and then use it in a way that creates the kind of changes they want. You can't do it *for* them. All hypnosis is self-hypnosis. You need to *tell* them this. Then you need to provide some convincing evidence that they *have* this power. This makes the participant responsible for the results.

If you don't make participants responsible for the results, they might find reasons to doubt that the hypnosis happened. That defeats your purpose. You need them to believe they took themselves into hypnosis. The way to do this is to use a convincer.

A simple eye-lock test can be used to convince the client that all hypnosis is self-hypnosis. The eye-lock test is a simple set of instructions to close the eyes, relax them to the point they won't work, and then *test* to make sure they won't work. This is a covert test. The client knows they are being tested. The trick is to *make sure* it's a test they cannot fail.

The purpose of the eye-lock test is to show the client that they're choosing to accept your suggestions and that by accepting your suggestions hypnosis will happen. This is how you make someone responsible for the results they're getting.

The following is a brilliant variation on the eye-lock test that works well for both individual sessions and group hypnosis sessions:[14]

First, guide the group to close their eyes. Follow this with the suggestion to relax the eyelids to the point where they won't work. Then, tell them to double the relaxation.

Now, here's the fail-safe suggestion. Give instructions to keep doubling the relaxation until *they're sure* that the eyelids *won't work*. Remind them - *I can't do it for you*. Then, let them know what failure means because some people are going to challenge your authority. Tell them, "If the eyelids were to open that would simply mean that you need to double the relaxation a few more times." Be really clear on this point - it's up to *them* to accomplish this because you can't do it for them.

To be successful, all they need to do is to keep doubling the relaxation until *they're satisfied* that the eyelids won't work. It's *when* they're sure that they're to test. Until they're sure, "keep doubling the relaxation." I like to add the suggestion, "You may find that the *eyebrows* go up and down. But the eyelids will lay flat and calm and completely relaxed." This allows you to see when each person is doing the test because their eyebrows will lift a little. I have never had this technique fail. So, don't be afraid to suggest to "test hard." You want that suggestion, "satisfy yourself that they just won't work" to carry weight. This will ensure that you have established reasonable expectations; your participants will understand that *they* are responsible for the results.

---

[14] I got this technique from the late stage hypnotist Raveen. He hypnotized hundreds of people at a time!

Make sure everyone in your group is successful before you move on to the next step. If someone opens their eyes, you'll see it. You can then smile and nod in a way that says, "That's right." Give them a non-verbal suggestion by waving your hand down to instruct them to close their eyes again. Then, repeat your instructions to the entire group. Just say, "Your eyes are closed," which is true. Then add, "So, let's just do that again." Repeat the instructions and have them do the test again. This will give the person who opened their eyes a second shot at being successful while compounding the response for everyone else, making it stronger. Nice, right?

The Patter

1. *Close the eyes.*
2. *Relax them to the point they won't work.*
3. *Test to make sure they won't work.*
4. *Now double the relaxation. That's right.*

Double the relaxation. Now, double it again. And again. And again. And keep doubling that relaxation until you're sure they won't work. Now, I can't do this for you. If the eyelids were to open that would simply mean that you need to double the relaxation a few more times, so keep doubling the relaxation until **you're satisfied** *that they just won't work. And when you're sure, go ahead and give them a little check.*

Relax the Body

Relaxation hypnosis utilizes suggestions for *physical* relaxation. Physical relaxation is not a guarantee of hypnosis. But in a group setting you don't have any way of testing for state. All you can do is give suggestions for deepening physical relaxation. Because the mind tends to follow the body, once you have established some measure of physical relaxation, continuing to deepen the awareness of feelings and sensations of relaxation in the body should result in the person entering into a light state of hypnosis.

Some of the deepening techniques that work well in a group setting are the deepening count, fractionating, and imagery. A deepening count can count up or down. Either way works. If you count UP, suggest going *more* deeply relaxed. If you count DOWN, suggest going deeper *down into* relaxation. Between each count, you can add some intermittent suggestions, if you like. For example – Ten … deeper down, deeper relaxed … Nine … relax, relax, relax … Eight … Deeper down. And as the body relaxes, deeper and deeper, the mind relaxes, more and more … and so on. Alternatively, you can also use a pregnant pause between counts. Silence is a great deepener.

Silence makes a better deepener once you have established some depth of hypnosis. I like to start out with intermittent suggestions because this teaches the client how to respond between each count. I want to keep giving suggestions to keep the conscious mind focused. I'll follow this with a second and even a third count, slowing the intervals, and using a pregnant pause between counts.

Fractionate

Fractionating is a deepening technique where the person opens the eyes and then closes the eyes, repeatedly. You can fractionate a person right down into hypnosis with this technique, but I don't recommend it. Some people find it very annoying. You want their first experience with you to be a positive one so, if you're going to use fractionating, only do it a few times. Then switch to another deepening technique.

Imagery

Another useful deepening technique is imagery. Because the subconscious mind speaks in pictures, any image you suggest is going to speak directly to a person's subconscious mind. In a group, you need to keep your suggestions generic. For example, "Imagine what it would be like to be twice as relaxed."

If you're planning to use guided imagery in a group session, you can set it up before you begin the induction process. Get out your whiteboard and facilitate a little preliminary uncovering process. Ask participants to give you examples of situations where they felt "totally calm and totally relaxed." For example, the feeling and sensations of floating comfortably in a warm bath. This "brainstorming" session only takes a few minutes, and it will give you more targeted imagery you can incorporate into the session. These are the imagined experiences that will be most effective for the people in your group.

Wrap Up Convincingly

Hypnosis itself doesn't feel like anything. The purpose of using suggestions for physical relaxation in a group session is to provide proof that the hypnosis happened. If you don't provide proof, some people will just be tempted to think, "Well, I felt relaxed but . . . I don't think I was hypnotized." You need them to be convinced that they were *hypnotized*. That's what they think they're paying for. What they're actually paying for are the results they can get *through* the hypnosis. But hypnosis isn't relaxation. You don't need any relaxation for hypnosis to happen. Remember, the benefit of using suggestions for *physical* relaxation is that you can then use it as a Convincer. Make the connection between the sensations of relaxation and the ability to enter the state of hypnosis and the client will realize, "*So that's* hypnosis!"

If participants have followed your instructions, by the end of the session they'll be feeling more relaxed than when they began. Before you emerge the group from hypnosis, take a moment to bring their awareness to these changes. This provides evidence of change. Give the suggestion, "In a moment, I'm going to (however you are going to emerge them)" Then give the instructions, "Take a moment to go inside and do a scan of the body. And just notice how much better you feel than when you began."

Any recognition of the difference between when they started, and the end of the session can be used as proof that change has occurred. These changes can then be tied to the ability to create positive changes using the power of the mind. Help them to realize just how quickly and easily they were able to let go of some of the stress and tension they were holding onto. This is the power of their own mind! After all, the only thing *you* have done is offer a few suggestions and *they* have created this experience of deepening relaxation. How did they do that? Easily. It's simply by following your instructions that they have created this deepening state of hypnosis. That's the convincer.

The purpose of a Convincer is to provide *proof* that something has happened. In this case, you're providing proof that the hypnosis happened. The purpose of the hypnosis is to create the kind of change they want. That's why the hypnosis *needs* to happen. Prove that it happened. Then tie it to the ability to create positive change.

In a private session, before emerging the client, I would invite them to go inside and *notice* what, if anything, has changed. Then, I would offer a suggestion in the form of a question, "Feel relaxed?" When the client responded to the affirmative, I would offer the following suggestions, "Notice how much better you feel. Realize, you did that! All *I* have done is deliver a few suggestions and *you* have relaxed yourself. Good

Ditch the Pitch!

job! Let yourself smile and mentally give yourself a pat on the back. You've done well!" Help your clients to *own* this wonderful ability they already have. Get them to celebrate it! Then tie it to their ability to feel better anytime they want to. Remind them, "*This* is the power of your subconscious mind. Realizing, it can make you into the kind of person you *want* to be. Feel proud!" Then give them a few moments of silence during which "all the positive suggestions and good feelings now sink to the deepest part of the mind . . ." Add a few post-hypnotic suggestions for general well-being, sleep, that sort of thing. Then emerge the group.

Now, here's the trick. *Immediately* after you emerge the group from hypnosis, direct their attention to a list of the more common signs of hypnosis, and ask, "Who experienced any of these?"

This does three things. First, it brings their attention back to you. Don't let them start talking amongst themselves. Keep their attention on you. You're not done yet.

Second, often what you'll hear is an expression of surprise. You'll hear, "*Oh!*" What this means is, "So *that's* hypnosis!" Continue to deliver suggestions to approve of their success because *they're not fully emerged yet*. There's a brief window after you emerge a person where the mind is still hyper-suggestible. Keep delivering the suggestions. Reinforce their ability to be successful using this powerful resource that they already have.

Third, if you have any skeptics in the group, they'll be surprised by the responses of everyone else. As a result, they won't be a problem.

Summary:

Be prepared to invest in tools and equipment that will support you in consistently teaching the same material from one class to another to ensure you're delivering a high-quality learning experience for all your students. For example, a notebook computer, projector, portable projector screen, whiteboard, dry-erase markers, CD player, extension cords, shipping tape, and tissues.

Make your presentation engaging by getting students involved while you deliver your content. Make sure the focus of your presentation is relevant to your specific topic.

Keep your presentation simple. Use bullet points, imagery, and colors to emphasize key points for students. Reference your notes to provide more details. Providing students with handouts will help to keep the focus on you.

Structure your class time to allow for frequent breaks. If students are going out for lunch, remember to allow extra time for the lunch break.

Structure your hypnosis session with a clear beginning and clear ending. Make participants responsible for the results by incorporating an overt test such as the eye-lock test. Then deepen with suggestions for physical relaxation. If you plan to utilize imagery, consider setting up before the session by facilitating a brainstorming session to gather imagery that would be most effective for your students.

Wrap up your session with a convincer. Remember, the purpose of delivering lots of suggestions for physical relaxation is to provide proof that change has happened. Before emerging your students from hypnosis, bring their attention to how much better they feel than when they began. Then, tie these changes to their ability to create the kinds of change they want. Remember, just because a person opened their eyes doesn't mean they have fully emerged from hypnosis. Immediately bring their attention to your list of "signs of hypnosis." Explain why these changes occur and they'll convince themselves that they did, indeed, experience hypnosis.

11 Common Signs of Hypnosis

1. Bloodshot eyes (most common) – Relaxation in the eyeball allows greater blood flow. The blood vessels dilate causing blood to rush into the white area of the eyeball.

2. Rapid Eye Movement (REM) – The eyeballs move back and forth behind the eyelids indicating visual activity is occurring.

3. Eye Roll (occurs in deeply relaxed states) – The eyes roll up and back in the sockets leaving only the whites showing.

4. Lacrimation – "Teary eyes" occurs when the tear-ducts relax to the point of watering involuntarily.

5. Salivation - Salivary glands may increase production of saliva in the mouth resulting in increased swallowing.

6. Eyelid flutter – As the muscles in the eyelid relax the nerves jump.

7. Muscle fasciculation – Twitching or jerks in the small muscles occur as the nervous system releases tension.

8. Body temperature – cold or warm, due to lower pulse rate or circulation of blood. Warm is the more common subjective experience. The client may also notice tingling sensations as blood flow increases.

9. Change in breathing – Breathing may be faster or slower. Deep sighs occur when the brain requires more oxygen to deal with a new or fearful situation, or when releasing stress.

10. Face Flushes – Increased circulation may result in blotchiness in face and neck. (More common with men.)

11. Lethargic, limp state – triggered by release of chemical relaxant from the brain (endorphins). The client may experience sensations of sinking or floating

CHAPTER 6:
Meet People

Holistic fairs are a fun way to meet people who might be interested in your services. It's a great venue for meeting people you like and for showcasing your fabulous self. It can be an effective way for you to get more clients! Meeting people in person will generate business for you. Just remember the goal is to get them to call you. If you just hand out your business card, you might not get that call. Come up with an incentive for people to call you to learn more.

The fees for a booth at a holistic fair can sometimes be quite costly. If you're just starting out and watching your expenses, this doesn't need to be a problem. Think about who you could share a booth with. Find someone in a complimentary business that you can share the cost with. For example, I shared a large corner booth at a two-day wellness fair with a new day-spa that was just starting up. We were not competing businesses and sharing the expense of a booth allowed us to pay a little extra to get a corner booth right next to the front entrance.

This worked out great for both of us by giving us a prime location with two frontages and lots of traffic. The spa used the side table to display their brochures and chat with prospective customers while the back area of the booth provided an area for a massage table. I used the front table for my display and handouts. Once set up, I just focused on meeting people, sharing my Who-What-How message, answering questions, handing out brochures, and inviting folks to get on my list to attend the upcoming introductory talk.

People who attend these events are looking for free bees. This means that you need to have something that you can give away. Ideally, it should be something that will bring them into your office. For example, I handed out tickets to an introductory talk I was giving shortly after the fair. This included the opportunity to experience a free group hypnosis session. There was also a dollar value printed on the face of the ticket, along with instructions to call to reserve their seat. Not only did I get a big turnout but, following the event, I got quite a few new clients! Some booked their first session right away. Others called a few days later. The stragglers took several months before picking up the phone to call me. But I got the call!

When you have a conversation with a passer-by, you can qualify those who would like to receive more information (or get access to a special gift). Keep a sign-up sheet on your table to collect names and contact information. If someone expresses interest in learning more, invite them to *print* their name, phone number, and email address on the sheet. After the event you'll have a list of prospective new clients. Just remember, it's your job to follow up. This will give you another opportunity to schedule them in for a discovery call, attend your presentation, or book their first session.

Some hypnotherapists hand out free CDs at holistic fairs. It's a lovely gift. The problem is that it's likely to get lost in the bottom of their goodie-bag. And there's little incentive for the person to call you, once they have the hypnosis session in hand. Maybe they'll listen to the recording. Maybe they won't. Either way, you're not getting the conversation.

If you want to give away a free audio recording, that's awesome! Just come up with a better strategy. For example, you could hand out tokens or gift certificates. This gives your prospects something tangible that they can put in their goodie bag. Unfortunately, it's probably going to get lost in the goodie-bag. You need to come up with a way to make whatever you're giving away *stand out*! A better option is to invite folks to visit your website to download a free audio recording.

If you require folks to opt-in to your mailing list to access their download this gives you another opportunity to start a conversation. (They can unsubscribe at any time.) They're giving you their email address in exchange for your gift. This legally gives you permission to contact them by email.[15] Once you have a person's email address, it's very easy for you to stay in touch. This is something that you can automate. Simply create a series of short, informative emails. Then schedule each email to go out every three to five days. Share information of value. Inform, educate, don't sell. That's what you're good at. Teach them something useful.

---

[15] You'll need to sign up for an email service for this. I use Get Response because it's relatively easy to use. They have lots of tutorials to support you. Plus you can create newsletters and automate emails.

When you put your message in your prospective client's inbox multiple times, you become familiar. Subconsciously, familiar is safe. Let them get to know you! Then, in the final email in your automated sequence, invite them to come in for a free discovery session, attend one of your free presentations, or sign up for your self-hypnosis course where they can learn some self-empowerment strategies.

It's Your Business

DO NOT leave your booth unattended. If you need to take a bathroom break, make sure you have someone to cover for you.

DO NOT have your kids, dog, girlfriends, or other distractions at your booth. Give your full attention to attracting clientele.

DO NOT give away free hypnosis sessions. Offer a free consultation by phone or in your office. Give out coupons as reminders. Better yet, schedule them in, then send them an email reminder.

DO NOT hang out in the corner pouring over someone's problems. Ask them for their number and arrange to call them at a more appropriate time.

BEST NOT to give out a hypnosis CD. Offer something that will bring them into your office. Remember, your promotional material will get buried in the goody-bag. If you want to make a lasting impression you need to have a conversation.

DO have brochures and business cards with you. Make sure your contact information is on all your handouts. Better yet, put your lovely face on all your marketing material. Smile! Look friendly.

Ditch the Pitch!

DO always dress and act professionally. Consider investing in a professional name tag with your name and business engraved on it. (Any trophy shop can provide this.)

DO invest in professional looking display material, cards and brochures. A local sign shop can make you banners, display cards and posters. If you have a flair for design, you can make your own cards and brochures at www.vistaprint.com

DO keep snacks and water on hand to keep your energy high. Having treats to hand out to passers-by can get you conversations. (Foil-wrapped chocolates are always a winner.)

DO be approachable. Stand up, smile, greet people. Be memorable. Remember your breath mints. : -)

DO give people a reason to contact you later. For example, expiry date on your offering, limited seating, etc.

DO give a presentation if you are given the opportunity to speak at the event. Prepare in advance and have a handout that goes with your talk. Remember to make it interactive!

DO give demonstrations of how quickly and easily a person can enter hypnosis and enjoy it (keep it under 5 minutes).

DO offer anyone you talk to a coupon toward something of value such as relaxation CD/recording, class, consult, etc.

DO collect contact information. Consider having a draw for a gift basket, book, coffee mug/card, CD, or a short stress-buster session. (Make it a yummy mind-massage experience!)

DO schedule a special educational presentation on hypnosis and (your specific topic) as a follow up.

DO give away free tickets to your post-fair presentation. Make sure it displays the date, contact info, and a value for the class or presentation.

DO include a free group hypnosis session in your free presentation.

DO have an opt-in or sign-up sheet for your newsletter, report, tip-list, or special gift.

DO be prepared for new business. Have a system in place so you can manage the sudden increase in traffic.

Summary:

Holistic Fairs are a fun way to meet people who are interested in learning more about what you do! If you're on a budget, consider sharing costs with a complimentary business.

Remember, everyone will have a goodie bag. Make sure you have plenty of handouts and come up with an incentive for people to call you.

If you have the opportunity to give a presentation at the fair, grab it! It will get you business.

Be professional, mingle and have fun. Be shiny!

CHAPTER 7:
Get Fairly Compensated

A common mistake many beginners make is offering discounts on sessions. It can seem like a reasonable thing to do when you're just starting out. You think, "I'm new at this!" You just want to get some warm bodies into your chair and discounting your rate can seem like a reasonable way to do that. But behind this reasoning lurks an emotional menace that says, "I'm not very *good* at this!" That's the voice of the Inner Saboteur convincing you that what you're offering isn't good enough. Big mistake.

The biggest problem with discounting your sessions is that, *subconsciously*, it says, "worth-less." This is not a suggestion you want to offer anyone - least of all yourself. So, don't discount - *ever*. To attract clients that you can be successful with you need to be seen in the right light. You need to be seen as the best choice – not the best bargain. This begins with valuing *yourself* and what you do. Remember - you need clients who are motivated, not just looking for the best deal.

You need clients who are highly motivated. The greater the client's motivation, the better your results are going to be. Discounting won't get you the results you're after because you can't *make* a person change. You can't do it for them. Besides, your investment in the results should never be greater than the clients'. If it is, you're sunk.

It took me five years to really grasp this - *the client is responsible for the results*. The power isn't in the hypnosis. The power is in the mind of the client. To access that power requires an investment of both time and money. *You* have already made the investment. But you can't do it for them. All you can do is guide the process. Remember, hypnotherapy requires a relationship. It's a partnership where you and the client work together to achieve their goal.

You can't do all the work. If you try, you'll fail. You'll end up struggling to get results, you'll work too hard, and you won't get paid what you're worth. While it's a temptation to discount your services when you're just starting out, discounting will only leave you feeling short-changed. Over time you'll start to resent your clients. That won't get them healed. Worse, if you don't love what you're doing, you're going to find it hard to invest in growing your practice.

When you are being fairly compensated for your services, you will gladly go that extra mile for your clients. That's what will get you stellar results. So really get this - you need to establish yourself as the best *choice* – not the best bargain. You need to be seen in the best light. The way to achieve this is to provide a superior service. That's what will allow you to charge a premium fee. But to do that you need to deliver your promise of results. You can't promise a one-session miracle because it's not up to you.

The client is responsible for the results. Most people don't turn to hypnosis as their first solution. That means, most people are going to need a process. Healing can take time. One of the ways you can give yourself and your client the time you need to get those results is to offer a multi-session package.

Session Packages

Instead of discounting your rate, offer an *incentive* for pre-paying and pre-scheduling a bundle of sessions ahead of time. For example, I offered a five-session package. The client paid for the first four sessions. The fifth session was free. It's not a discount. It's a *reward* for committing to a program. Everyone understands the benefits of buying in bulk. That's why Costco is such a huge success.

Promoting a package will make your job so much easier. First, you get payment up front which means you have a committed client.

Second, don't have to collect payment every session. This gets the business out of the way right up front which frees you up to focus on resolving the client's issue. That's what they're paying you for, right?

Third, it allows you to schedule your time weeks in advance. This gives you a sense of control over your time and allows you to plan. Having clients scheduled ahead of time will boost your confidence. It will keep you feeling invested in growing your business.

Finally, when a person calls to inquire about your services, you can honestly say that you're booked weeks in advance. This increases your credibility and desirability. Obviously, you're in demand!

The biggest benefit of pre-selling a package of sessions is that it puts clients in your chair who are committed to a healing program. A committed client is a person who is invested in getting the results they're after. They're motivated to do the work required to get those results. That's your ideal client. The more motivated a person is, the better your results will be. When a client commits to a healing program it gives you the time *you* need to get lasting results.

These are the clients that are going to help you to grow your healing practice. Successful clients will sing your praises and send you referrals. So instead of discounting your services, come up with a session package you can offer. Give your clients incentives for investing in a program and you'll get better results.

Coupon Deals

Coupons might be a way for you to promote your hypnosis practice provided you have a clear marketing strategy in mind. If you don't, it could end up costing you. You just need to be clear about what your purpose for offering a coupon deal is. Coupon deals are an effective way to get more clients if you're just starting out. It's *not* a way to make money.

Online Coupon Deals is *no-cost marketing*. There's no out-of-pocket expense involved in advertising your product or services. But you still must invest the same amount of time and effort to do the work - and with very little return. If you're looking for a way to make money – this ain't it! Coupon companies offer deep discounts on valuable products and services. The provider of those goods or services receives a percentage of the proceeds. You will earn something for your time but it's slave wages.

For the most part, people who buy coupons are in it for the deal. They're bargain hunters. They're not going to want to pay your full session fee once they've received the service at a discount rate.

If you want a way to gain experience and build your skills working with a lot of different clients, this might be worth considering.

If you need testimonials for your website and marketing material, this might be an effective way to get some. But it's up to you to make this a condition of the deal. And you'll need to have a system and be diligent about collecting them.

Coupons can be an effective way to introduce a new product or discount on an existing product that would otherwise be a loss such as airfare; hotel stays; group tours; kayak rentals; etc.

Coupon deals are also suited to selling low-cost or no-cost products. Examples of low-cost products include "widgets" of any sort; toys; electronic accessories. An example of a no-cost product is digital downloads.

The hypnotist, Raveen, offered a coupon deal on his Gastric By-Pass Hypnosis program which included a couple of e-books and a series of hypnosis CD's. The whole package was valued at $400 discounted down to $97 as "the deal."

If you want to make money through coupon offers you need to either:

1. Create a digital product and offer it at a significant discount.
2. Convert your coupon purchaser into a regular client.

Think Before You Act

Coupon deals *might* be a way for you to promote your hypnosis practice *provided* you have a clear marketing strategy in mind. But you need to think carefully before you act. The following two examples of coupon deals illustrate different approaches. Both were healing practitioners using coupon deals to get more clients. One was a disaster. The other created a repeat clientele.

Disaster

The first coupon offer was for a 90-minute shiatsu massage for $49. Good deal, right?

Unfortunately, it was a marketing disaster.

Here's why. The massage therapist scheduled the coupon-client in for their massage. She provided the service. She *hoped* that doing a good job would convince them to come back. They didn't. As a result, she failed to grow her clientele base. I know this because I bought one of her deals. Several months later, we met at a business networking meeting, and I asked her how well her coupon deal had paid off. She said she got a terrific response. She was very busy for several weeks. And then … crickets.

She couldn't figure it out. Everybody claimed to love her service. Why weren't these people booking more sessions with her? I'll answer this question in a minute. But this is a good example of how *not* to use coupons to promote your healing practice. Based on this model you'd be working for about $16 an hour, which hardly compensates you for your investment in training.

Ka-Ching!

The second coupon offer was also for a massage. It was a 60-minute massage for $49. Also, a good deal! Like the first massage therapist, the practitioner scheduled the coupon-client in for their massage. But here's where the similarities end.

This therapist had a system in order to establish a relationship with each new client. First, she emailed confirmation of the appointment with directions to her office. When the client came in, she provided the service, as promised. Then, at the end of the session she offered the client a choice of two different multi-session packages.

This is a smart marketing strategy. It's smart because the client has *already* invested in the service. As a result, they're more likely to buy. Following the treatment, they're feeling great. What better time to offer them the opportunity to feel great again by continuing to enjoy the service? I know because I bought a package.

While these two massage services were a little different, the coupon deals offered are comparable. Both therapists were offering a massage. But that's where the similarities end. Their approaches to marketing a healing practice were very different.

The first therapist was focused on the practice. She was focused on doing a good job and delivering a good service. There's nothing wrong with that. She got lots of new clients, too. The problem is that these were single-session clients. They were only there for the deal. And she didn't have any strategy in place to convert them into clients.

The second massage therapist was focused on growing her healing practice. She got lots of new clients, too. These were single-session clients, too. But she had a strategy for converting them into repeat, *paying* clients. When a person signed up for the single-session deal, she had a follow-up system in place. When she delivered the service, she had a way to convert them into long-term clients.

The first session only paid her about $25 for the hour. But her package deal got her more clients. It put more ka-ching in her jeans. Because she was only discounting the first session to attract new clients, this strategy paid off. She had to share the proceeds of the first session with the coupon company. But after that, it was pure profit. This approach also got her committed clients who were scheduled in for sessions weeks in advance.

This is the difference between "doing" hypnotherapy and running a hypnotherapy *business*. It's all in how you think about it. If you don't have a strategy for converting a single session into a client, it doesn't matter that you provide an exceptional service. If you leave it up to the client to come back, they probably won't. They'll get busy and forget all about you. Once the rush is over, it will be just you and the crickets.

What's Your WIIFM?

Before offering a deal, get very clear about your WIIFM. What's in it for you? A coupon deal might be the way to get more clients. Or it could cost you. If you're just starting out and need more experience, this might be what you're looking for. You'll get clients who have some financial investment in the results. You'll get lots of practice with a variety of people. You'll pocket a little ka-ching. All good.

If you need more clients, coupon deals *might* be a way to get them. Just make sure it's the best deal for *you*. Then make sure you have a strategy to convert a single-session, bargain-hunting "customer" into a repeat client who is willing to pay your fee.

Summary:

To attract new clientele, you need to be seen in the right light. You need to be seen as the best choice – not the best bargain. Instead of discounting your valuable services, focus on providing a superior service. That's what will allow you to charge a premium fee.

You can't promise a one-session miracle because the *client* is responsible for the results. Healing can take time. Offering a multi-session package can give your client the time they need to allow the healing to happen.

Online Coupon Deals can be a way to attract new clients provided you have a marketing strategy in mind. Most people buy coupons for the deal. If you don't have a strategy for converting them from a single session into a client, it won't matter how exceptional your service is.

Online Coupon Deals is *no-cost marketing*. There's no out-of-pocket expense involved in advertising your product or services. You will earn something for your time but it's slave wages.

A Coupon Deal might be an effective way for you to promote your business. The question you need to ask yourself is, What's in it for *me*?

A Coupon Deal offer might be worth considering *if*. . .

- You want a way to gain experience and build your skill working with a lot of different clients
- You need testimonials for your website and marketing material
- to introduce a new product (e.g. digital)

If you decide to make use of a Coupon Offer, make sure you have a strategy for getting that testimonial or turning a bargain-hunter into repeat clientele.

While coupon deals aren't a way to make money, they could be a good way to get testimonials. Offer a low-cost experience of hypnotherapy. Then, ask for a testimonial. Make it a condition of the deal. Remember, it's up to you to collect your client's testimonials once you have delivered the service. Make sure you have a strategy for doing that before you make the offer.

CHAPTER 8:
Get Great Testimonials

Testimonials are a great way to promote your healing practice. But to use them effectively to attract clients you need to understand what they're for. The purpose of a testimonial is not to blow your own horn. It's not to sell a person on hypnosis. It's to convince folks who are already interested in hypnosis that *you* are the best choice for them. The easiest way to prove that you're the best choice is to let other people blow your horn for you. This is what testimonials do.

A testimonial is an unbiased recommendation for your services. A well-crafted testimonial will help you to get more clients. But they need to come from *real clients* - not your mom, your best friend, and your spouse. (They know you and love you. But let's face it - they're biased.)

There are two mistakes you can make when it comes to testimonials. The first mistake is having no testimonials at all. The second mistake is using testimonials that praise how wonderful you are - which is true. But they won't speak to anyone but you.

When you help a person get rid of their problem, they'll love you. They'll love to say so in their testimonial. But the best testimonials aren't about you. They're about the person reading them.

Testimonials of love and appreciation will make *you* feel terrific. But they won't attract new clients. This is because a person who considers your services has only one question on their mind – their WIIFM. The only thing they want to know is, "*Can you help me get rid of this problem?*" Who can better answer that question than someone you helped to overcome that problem?

The Best Testimonials

Testimonials are real clients recommending you to others. The best testimonial is going to offer a before and after picture. This helps to offer proof to the reader that it's worth it to them to pick up the phone and call you – NOW. That's the essential purpose of your client-attraction system, right?

The best testimonials communicate three things.

1. *Who* you helped (a real person)
2. *What* problem they were struggling with (specifically)
3. *How* you helped them be successful (before/after)

Testimonials speak to a person when they're undecided. If they're on the fence about whether you are the answer that they've been looking for, a great testimonial can be the deciding factor. A Who-What-How testimonial tells the reader *why* you are the best choice for them. It can convince them that it's worth it to pick up the phone and call you.

A testimonial that says, *"Barry's a great guy!"* or *"Mary is super!"* won't do that. You need to be more strategic with testimonials. Your testimonials should tell the reader how *they* might benefit from working with you.

The best testimonial reads like a story. It gives a before and after snapshot of the person you helped. If the person you helped had the same problem as the reader, they're going to want to read more. They're going to want to know - what happened? What changed? What was it like working with you? They'll also be interested to hear what *surprised* your client about the process, especially if your client had some apprehension about the process at first.

They might like to hear how your approach is different from other approaches your client has tried. This could speak to someone who tried hypnosis in the past but didn't get a lasting result. It could convince them to try it again. They'll also be interested in discovering what other benefits they might receive from the process. For example, clients often have some unexpected side-benefits such as sleeping better, losing weight, or feeling confident in other situations. This makes for a great testimonial.

How to Get Great Testimonials

Your best client attractor – bar none - is always going to be your ability to deliver real and lasting results. When you deliver on your promises to your clients, they'll gladly return the favor by providing you with a testimonial. All you have to do is ask them for one. Then, make it easy for them by giving them a feedback form they can fill out.

Create a feedback form.

When you complete a healing program with a client, ask them to fill out a feedback form. On one side of the form, offer a list of questions that can be answered in a sentence or two. Leave space between each question so the client can express their thoughts fully.

The following is the feedback form I used in my practice. Customize it to your needs and you'll have everything you need for great testimonials you can use to promote your practice.

--- Your Feedback is Important! ---

You have just completed a process of self-healing and self-empowerment using hypnosis. Please take a few moments to share your experience of hypnotherapy. Thanks, again, for allowing me to be your guide!

1. Describe the benefits/results you are enjoying from working together.

2. Describe the problem that brought you to hypnotherapy.

3. Describe what changes have occurred and how this has impacted your daily life.

4. The three most significant improvements I am enjoying . . .

5. If someone questions the value of [your name/business] hypnosis services, would you be available to answer their questions? Yes _____ No _____

Name:

Email:

Phone:

I give permission [insert your Name] to share this information:

_____
(Signature)

If you would like to comment further, please use the other side of this page. Thank you!

Note: You need consent to use a person's feedback as a testimonial. Make sure you include a place for their signature giving you permission to use their comments. If possible, get permission to use their name. This adds credibility to your testimonial. (If you're specializing in weight loss, before and after photos are your best-sellers.)

On the other side of the form, provide a space for the client to write you a letter. Be sure to give some suggestions on how best to structure their letter. For example:

> **--- Write me a feedback letter! ---**
>
> *Here are a few suggestions to help you get started:*
>
> 1. This is the problem I came to see you about . . .
> 2. What was your life like before hypnotherapy?
> 3. This is what I experienced and how it changed me . . .
> 4. These are some of the benefits I am now enjoying . . .
> 5. What surprised me the most was . . .
> 6. Why I would recommend you to my friends . . .
> 7. Anything else?

Eliminate excuses.

Some clients prefer to write something for you at home. They want time to reflect and give you their honest opinion. In this case, give them an addressed, stamped envelope. This will ensure that there are no excuses. Once a person gets back to daily life they'll forget about you. If you haven't received their feedback form within a week or two, don't take it personally. Follow up with a phone call or an email. If they agreed to give you their testimonial hold them to their word.

I've had clients forget to return their completed testimonial to me. 99% of the time they had completed it like a homework assignment. They just forgot to post it. Make sure you follow up because there's gold in feedback forms.

Make a trade.

When you're just starting out, you may not have clients that you can ask for testimonials. This doesn't have to be an obstacle. If you have time to spare, make a trade for a testimonial. Come up with a list of people you know that you can help. Make sure they're a good fit for you. Then offer to do a trade in exchange for them writing you a testimonial.

This is a real win-win because it gives you the opportunity to get more experience working with real clients. Your clients will get the opportunity to learn more about themselves while doing some high quality self-healing work - all for the price of sharing their experience with others. Not only does this get you testimonials you can use to promote your services, but you may also convert your trades into paying clients. In this case, offer them a reduced rate to continue working with you. Better yet, offer them an incentive to send you referrals.

I have a friend who built a thriving practice on a referral program. She offered her clients a free session for every referred client who signed up for a three-session package. It was like a coffee-card! Within six months, she was booked so far in advance that she had to discontinue the offer. She was just too busy to continue the referral program.

Support a charity.

Another place you can do an exchange for testimonials is through a local charity. For example, I used to work for Hospice. We had a weekly self-care clinic where healing sessions were provided for volunteers and clients. The clinic was a big hit with a steady stream of clients lined up to receive their free session.

This is the one situation where I would like to offer free services. The people who so generously volunteer their services are the unsung heroes in the community. They show up tirelessly to give of themselves without expectation of payment. They deserve a reward. You can give them one by trading generosity for generosity.

Just pick a charity you'd like to support and see if they're open to sending you volunteers for healing sessions. Trade time for testimonials. You'll get lots of experience working with all kinds of people. Plus, you'll become known as the hypnosis expert – which will get you more clients.

You choose what you use.

The following are examples of testimonials clients have given me. I have left these unedited to allow you to see for yourself how you might choose to use all or part of a testimonial for marketing purposes.

Not every comment is necessarily going to be useful for marketing purposes. But it's always nice to receive a little praise and recognition. You can pull out the sections that answer your prospective client's most burning question – *Can you help me get rid of this problem?* A good testimonial will offer a resounding YES!!!

Hypnosis? Never again!

When I was an undergraduate, I was working on a paper on hypnosis and thought that the best way to learn about it was to experience it for myself. I went to a fellow who called himself a hypnotist but clearly did not understand much about the psyche because it was a frightening experience.

I was turned off of hypnosis for a long time after that. Until I met Wendie. She helped me to understand what hypnosis is and what it isn't, but most importantly to me – I trusted her. Because of that trust, I cautiously agreed to some hypnotherapy, and I'm so glad I did. She helped me reach places that I am overjoyed to have been. It was a brilliant step along the path to my own healing and growth. I am grateful and fortunate to have had such an experience, and such a trustworthy, professional guide.

Hypnotherapy has given me back my life.

Hypnotherapy helped me get my life back on track in a more confident, relaxed manner. Depression, stress, and guilt that ruled my life have been eliminated. I now sleep through the night, have clarity of mind. I now have the tools to handle stressful situations of everyday life in a new and positive manner. Problem-solving is a breeze. Life is now a total joy. I am able to cope with difficult situations with ease. I am more open and expressive. I am at peace with my Soul. Bonus – I dropped a pant size! Hypnotherapy has enriched my quality of life more than I could ever imagine possible.

Indecision and Self-Doubt

As Forrest Gump would say, "Life is like a box of chocolates; you never know what you're gonna get 'til you look inside." I have been given the gift to personally pick MY perfect box of chocolates – Chocolate-Mint and Carmel-filled milk chocolate!

I know now that I am fully capable of creating my own vision and executing it with perfect clarity. I've emptied my box (brain) of all unwanted chocolates (feelings, emotions and thoughts) and filled it up with all the things that fulfill me.

In no way am I saying life is a smooth path filled with ease, but I am saying that I have turned my valleys into peaks with the tools that Wendie has given me. I can make decisions based on my true, honest integrity and be proud of them.

I know I am a good person; I know I am fully capable and I know I am loved. I am me and proud of it. I know what is in my "box of chocolates" and I am perfectly happy with it.

I know I can face what is in front of me, now. Wendie has opened the doors to my clarity which helps me every day in appreciating my accomplishments and who I am.

Wendie, I love you and hold your teachings close to my heart in my everyday life. I would be who I am today without you.

Weight Loss

It's amazing how quickly we humans adapt. The changes I've gone through over the last months are incredible, but I have to think about it to be able to put it down.

When I started hypnotherapy, my goal was to lose weight, nothing else, really. What I've actually gotten out of it, is so much deeper. While my weight isn't much different, I am . . . to the core. Even to the point that my weight is no longer the issue it was when I started. Through hypnotherapy, I've become a happier person. I can recognize now the joy in little things that I didn't see before. It was as though I was looking through a dirty window then, and now the window has been thrown open to let in the daylight and sunshine.

I've also become more confident in my abilities, my strength and my own faith. When I saw the difference this therapy made in my daughter I felt I could also benefit. Seeing an 18-year-old angry, hostile girl become a self-assured, joyous and capable young woman living on her own, supporting herself and planning for her future, was undeniable proof that it produces positive results.

What a wonderful journey it's been. I embraced it fully, even when I felt afraid. The rewards are countless and wonderful. I highly recommend Wendie Webber and Mind Design Hypnosis to anyone seeking a more fulfilling, more peaceful life.

Self-Hypnosis Training

I had no qualms about being treated with hypnotherapy but was unsure as to what effect it would have. After the initial feeling of "trying something new", and "helping myself" had subsided, I was beginning to notice how much lighter and happier I felt.

The most important feeling I have is that there's no going back to that state of pent-up anger and sadness. The "low level infection" is gone. If it tries to creep back,

I'll know how to deal with it. Understanding what feelings are and how they operate makes life so simple. Much of what happened to me was self-imposed. The "stinkin' thinkin'" is laughable now. It is, however, an ongoing process and personal responsibility is important. I would recommend either private sessions or 7th Path to anyone.

Cancer

Don't kid yourself; hypnosis with Wendie Webber is work. It is also extremely worthwhile, and I am glad I committed to the process. While undergoing aggressive chemotherapy for (aggressive) breast cancer I thought hypnosis might help. It did.

A large part of the work done in hypnosis had to do with forgiveness. I had a hunch that the key to my ongoing health was the necessity to forgive my ex-husband and others who had put me in harm's way. Reading, talking, praying, being prayed for all contributed to my understanding of forgiveness. However, it was through Wendie's hypnosis sessions that I finally could access a true feeling of forgiveness "in my gut". This is no small thing.

It has been ten years since I finished chemotherapy. I am back at work, feeling healthy, hearty and whole. Life is good! Wendie knows true healing, and it is with love and joy that I recommend her to anyone who is sick and/or stuck. Thanks Wendie!

Creatively Blocked Songwriter

Thank you so much for your time last Saturday. The hypnotherapy session was incredible. It opened doors that had been closed to me for a long time. This past week, I have reflected on what we discussed and uncovered.

I have since purchased a ticket to go and see my Nanny in England. I will be going by myself, and I hope to just sit with her and talk. Thank you for showing me this is part of what I need to do. I am very excited about seeing her again.

I have also realized where my thoughts and emotions are coming from in my songwriting. I think, if anything, I understand myself a lot more. I think I know a little more about why I am the way I am. As it was a very intense session, I'm sure my understanding of my hypnotherapy session is just beginning. Thanks again.

"Eating for Comfort - Completely Out of Hand"

I first approached Wendie for help with a weight problem that I've had for some time. Wendie was very warm and soothing from the first moment and I'm sure that that was what kept me from running screaming out the door. I'm very guarded and seldom share any personal thoughts with anyone. I immediately felt that I could trust her with every word that I spoke, hypnotized or not.

What Wendie did was to make me understand that there are underlying reasons for most anything that we do as humans. My self-destructive behavior seems to have been based on childhood incidents that made me want to eat for comfort. That situation was completely out of hand before I met Wendie.

Through our sessions she kept peeling away the layers to get to the core of my subconscious need to over-eat. We have found that childhood trauma (real or imagined) had caused resentment towards many of my siblings that I carried with me for many years.

I'm not sure how much you want to hear but let me say that I recently had a weekend with some of my family and it was the best visit I have ever had with any of them. I've changed.

Wendie has also taught me some self-hypnosis techniques that have proven very helpful to me in many scenarios. As a practitioner, Wendie has done wonders for me and my everyday state of mind.

The weight is not completely off, yet. It's going slowly, but Wendie's therapy has "stopped the bleeding" and I feel much more in control of my eating habits. I am happier in life and for that I thank Wendie immensely. I feel that they just don't come any better than Wendie.

A Very Orthodox Guy - An Unorthodox Approach

A few years ago, in my mid-forties, I found myself struggling with life. Lots of things just weren't making sense. No surprise, there, I suppose. It seems to happen to a lot of us.

I am very reserved and independent about dealing with personal issues and so it took some time before I felt comfortable enough to work with Wendie, one on one, using hypnosis, to try to find my way through my malaise. I was treading new ground and if I said I wasn't scared I'd be lying to you. A very orthodox guy was taking an unorthodox approach.

Wendie was beautiful. She was completely at ease and comfortable with anything that we broached, and I found myself becoming more relaxed than I had been in years. I quite liked the whole experience of being in a state of hypnosis and it wasn't like anything I imagined hypnosis to be.

A few years later, I got an opportunity to take part in a 7th Path course that was conducted by Wendie. That course altered my life. I found peace, happiness, and confidence in a situation that had only brought out the opposite in the past. I simply applied what I learned in the course. Once again, Wendie was beautiful! I had never seen her work with a group before. Her ease with herself and the things she was presenting us set the tone for the whole course and left all of us wanting more. Witnessing that has been a rare experience in my life.

It's been a few years since the course, and I've had the privilege of being someone's sounding board numerous times. Every once in a while, I find someone who's really struggling with stuff, hard stuff, and I know I can't really do much more than give them love and encouragement to carry on . . . but I know someone who can . . . and so I've passed along Wendie's phone number to quite a few of them. I wouldn't hesitate to pass it on to you!

Answer the Burning Questions

The key to using a written testimonial is to answer the burning questions. When a testimonial answers the following four questions, they'll speak directly to your ideal clients.

1. **What problem was the person struggling with?** In other words, "This is the problem I came to see you about." Example: "*I first approached Wendie for help with a weight problem that I've had for some time.*"

2. **What changed as a result of working with you?** In other words - "This is what I experienced and how it changed me." Examples: *What Wendie did was make me understand that there are underlying reasons for most anything that we do as humans. My self-destructive behavior seems to have been based on childhood incidents that made me want to eat for comfort. That situation was completely out of hand before I met Wendie.*

   I found myself becoming more relaxed than I had been in years. I quite liked the whole experience of being in a state of hypnosis and it wasn't like anything I imagined hypnosis to be.

3. **What benefits are they now enjoying?** In other words, "These are some of the benefits I am now enjoying." Examples: *We have found that childhood trauma (real or imagined) had caused resentment towards many of my siblings that I carried with me for many years. I recently had a weekend with some of my family and it was*

the best visit I have ever had with any of them. I've changed. I feel much more in control of my eating habits. I am happier in life ...

4. **What made picking up the phone worth it?** In other words, "Why I would recommend you to my friends." Examples: *...has done wonders for me and my everyday state of mind.*

Seeing an 18-year-old angry, hostile girl become a self-assured, joyous and capable young woman living on her own, supporting herself and planning for her future, was undeniable proof that it produces positive results.

Every once in a while, I find someone who's really struggling with stuff, hard stuff, and I know I can't really do much more than give them love and encouragement to carry on . . . but I know someone who can . . .

Summary:

The purpose of a testimonial is not to sell a person on hypnosis. It's not to crow about how wonderful you are. It's a smart client-attraction strategy that provides proof that *you* are the best choice for resolving a specific problem a person is struggling with.

The best testimonial isn't about you. It's about the person who is reading it and *why* you are the best choice for them.

To get a great testimonial you must ask for it. You need to make it easy for clients to give you the information you need. The easiest way to do this is to create a feedback form that tells them what questions to answer and how to structure their comments.

A good testimonial is a story. It's about a real person with a real problem that you helped to be successful. That's a credible witness to the magic you do. Remember, word-of-mouth marketing is the gold standard. It costs you nothing. And it *will* get you more clients.

Your testimonials need to answer four most important questions.

1. What problem was the person struggling with?
2. What changed as a result of working with you?
3. What benefits are they enjoying now, as a result?
4. Why would they recommend you to others?

CHAPTER 9:
Get Started – Get Paid

When I was first starting out in my practice, I took a lot of courses and acquired a lot of tools and techniques. While I had a ton of enthusiasm for diving into the session work, I had no idea how to use everything that I had learned in a way that got real results. I only knew the "how to" of inductions, and deepeners, and therapeutic techniques – not the "why" behind them. This caused me problems in the session room.

It didn't take long for me to realize that "real" clients don't come in textbooks, they rarely follow the protocol, and the subconscious mind can zig when you tell it to zag. If you don't know what to do when that happens, it can really suck the confidence right out of you. If you're lacking in experience, having a few successes under your belt can do wonders to bolster your confidence. Here's an easy strategy you can use to get some clients into your chair without any pressure of having to prove anything.

Conduct a Study

Let your friends know that you're doing a study and that you need a few volunteers to work with. You can even charge a small fee. That's what I did when I finished training in Reconnective Healing. I partnered up with a fellow RH practitioner to conduct a "study" over three weekly sessions for which we charged $99. Good deal, right?

Following each session, the client would fill out a feedback form, describing what they experienced during the session. Then, when they came back in for the next session, they would give a report of what happened between sessions. After the third session, they were asked for a written testimonial. Do you see what this gives you? It's a fun way for you to gain some experience while developing your knowledge and skill working with multiple sessions.

A single session won't teach you much. Nor will it give you time to test the results. A three-session package gives you enough time to observe responses. It will allow you to test your results between sessions. Plus, you can ask for a testimonial at the end. Remember, when it comes to marketing your services, the gold standard is a testimonial from a satisfied customer.

Conducting a "study" means you don't have to make promises you can't keep. You're not promising to fix a problem. However, your goal should always be to deliver a result. Make a list of issues you feel confident that you can get a noticeable improvement with over a few sessions. Then, clearly communicate that these are the issues you're willing to include in your "study." For example, if you stick to surface issues, you're more likely to get a positive outcome.

People who notice *any* improvement are going to be intrigued. This can get you clients! Many will ask if they can continue working with you. Not only will this bolster your confidence, but you may also even surprise and amaze yourself with the results!

If you offer participants a special introductory session package after completing the study, many will take you up on it. They're already in the habit of coming to see you. Encourage them to continue that behavior by taking advantage of your special offer. Simple, right?

How to Set Up

First, set up your systems ahead of time. That way, you can test your systems out with real clients, free of the pressure of having to produce a result. This allows you to relax a little while you trial-run your system to make sure it's working for you. This can help you to feel more confident when you start accepting clients who are paying for your services. You'll have systems in place to support you. You'll have tested them in real sessions with real clients. You'll be able to tweak things, so that they work for you. And you'll be organized and ready to go to work when you start taking on paying clients.

Second, let folks know what to expect. What will they experience? What's the WIIFM? For example, the participants in my study were very excited about experiencing Reconnective Healing. Every participant had an issue that they wanted to "work on." And as practitioners, we were curious to see what, if any, the results might be. That was essentially "the contract."

Third, decide how many applicants you're going to accept into your study. If you limit the number of applicants, it creates a sense of urgency. This can ensure that folks aren't putting off signing up for their sessions. They'll be calling you and begging you to include them.

Limiting the number of participants also means that you won't be overwhelmed by too many clients all at once. You need time to review your sessions so you can think and strategize and plan.

Fourth, make sure you give yourself enough time to get some results. It may be "just" a study, but the goal is still to get a result. Decide on the number of sessions, then get a commitment from your trial clients to show up for their scheduled appointments. Better yet ask for a commitment is in cash. Get payment up front. Even if it's just a nominal fee – like $99 – it gives you a client who has an investment in the results. People who pay – pay attention. They're also more likely to show up and to receive benefit from the process.

Finally, create a feedback form/questionnaire for clients to fill out at the end of the study. This gives you a way to gather testimonials you can use to attract new clients into your practice. Remember to make sure that you have the client's permission to use their feedback for marketing purposes. For example, for the Reconnective Healing study, I created a simple protocol based on three sessions. The first session involved four steps.

1. The first step was to establish a therapeutic goal for each client. We needed to know what issue they were focusing on. We also needed to establish a baseline so we could measure the results.
2. The second step was to establish a therapeutic contract with the client. This involved educating the client about the process and establishing the rules about what to expect, and what to do and not do.
3. The third step was the healing session. This was just a short energy healing session – about 40 minutes. All the client had to do was relax and notice any feelings or sensations that

occurred during the session. They would then give a report following the session.

4. The fourth step was the post-session debriefing. Following the healing session the client would give feedback about what came up during the session.

At the end of the first session, the client was all set up for the next session. When they came back for their second session, the session started with a preliminary check-in. What we wanted to know was - what happened following their session? As you can see, this is just a continuation of the feedback process.

We then conducted the second healing session, same as before, which was followed with another post-session debriefing to collect feedback about the session.

The third and final session started with a preliminary check-in to see what had happened between sessions. This was followed by the third healing session. The post-session debriefing was then followed by the client filling out a feedback form with a series of questions on it. What we wanted to know is ...

- What was the experience like for them?
- How did they benefit?
- What surprised them about the process?
- Would they recommend you to others?

As you can see, we were constantly testing the results by getting feedback from the client throughout the process. We wanted to know what they experienced during the session, what happened following the session, and whether they were experiencing any side-effects. What we found is that people were experiencing positive results! Not only was this very exciting, but it was bolstering our faith in the process. But I also had an ulterior motive for conducting the study. I wanted to answer the question: *What happens when you put a person into somnambulism before you do the energy work?* I wanted to know how hypnosis might impact a person's healing process when combined with energy work.

Because there were two Reconnective Healing practitioners, I had the perfect opportunity to establish a control group. The clients who worked with my colleague got the standard Reconnective Healing Session. The clients I worked with also got Reconnective Healing, but before beginning the process, I guided the client into a state of somnambulism. And I discovered something very interesting. What I found was that the induction was unnecessary. The energy itself induced hypnosis. It happened very quickly, too. This turned out to be a very useful experience for me because it taught me that hypnosis happens. You just have to watch for it.

Years later, I got confirmation while attending a presentation given by a group of Chinese scientists at the National Guild of Hypnotists (NGH) Convention. The scientists were conducting a serious study into the use of acupuncture in Traditional Chinese Medicine. Acupuncture is where they place tiny needles into meridian points of the body.

The meridian system is a map of energy pathways throughout the body. Wherever these meridians intersect there is a point. When there's a block in the energy system, placing acupuncture needles at these meridian points can help to unblock the flow of energy or "chi". The purpose of all energy-based approaches to healing is to free up the energy needed to heal. Opening the meridian points allows the blocks to be released from the energy system. This frees up the energy the body needs to heal itself.

Well, something these scientists discovered – and it really surprised them - is that, when a person is in a state of somnambulism, the points in the meridian system open automatically. It happens naturally. (They even photographed this phenomenon.) When a meridian point is open you don't need to use needles! You can just touch the point, and it will respond. That's acupressure, which is the predecessor to acupuncture some four or five thousand years ago.

Now, if you're an EFT practitioner, you'll find this interesting because tapping induces hypnosis. The deeper a person goes into hypnosis, the more receptive the energy system of the body becomes. When a person is in somnambulism, you don't need to use a lot of pressure to get a release. You can just touch or gently rub a point. I found that just imagining or visualizing tapping on a point can get good results.

Summary:

Single sessions won't teach you much. But if you're inexperienced facilitating multiple sessions, an easy way to begin developing your own multi-session system is to conduct a study. You can use it to test your system, build your confidence, and gather testimonials you can use to promote your services. You can even get paid – without any pressure to produce a specific result.

Remember . . .

Hypnosis is not the answer — you are. That's what you're selling. There's more to hypnotherapy than inductions, deepeners, and therapeutic techniques. Much more.

Clients don't pay for hypnosis. They pay for the results. To get those results you need to feel confident working with the deeper issues. That's where the business lies.

You don't need more clients. Your ability to deliver results consistently is how you'll establish yourself as a unique service. It's how you'll be recognized as an expert and become known as the 'go-to' person for healing. That will attract more clients to you.

CHAPTER 10:
Keep in Contact

According to Webster's dictionary, a client is someone who comes under your care, protection and guidance. Think about that. You need to *care* about your clients and how well they're doing. A client-centered approach ensures that the focus is always on *the client* – not the technique. This is why it's so important to select your clients very carefully. It's because you're going to be asking that person to *let* you guide them through the underworld of their subconscious mind.

For many people the subconscious is a dark and scary place. It's filled with all sorts of unknowns and disowned Parts of them. Your primary job as a hypnotherapist is to protect the client while guiding them through the healing process. That's what's aligned with the subconscious mind's Prime Directive of self-preservation. You cannot override this. The subconscious mind *must* protect us. You need to work *with* this powerful directive by ensuring that it is *safe* for your clients to go where you need them to go, and do what you need them to do, to achieve their desired outcomes.

A Relationship Based on Trust

The healing process requires a relationship based on trust. This begins with establishing a therapeutic contract with the client[16] because *you can't do it for them.* You can't do what you need to do to guide the client to their success if the client is not willing to cooperate. Being client centered means making it safe for *the client* to take the next step.

Your job is simply to make it safe for the client to follow your instructions. If what you're asking the client to do is perceived as *not* safe, their subconscious mind is going to put up a block. That's its job. But this will prevent change from happening. For some reason, their subconscious mind feels that it is necessary to hold onto the problem.

This is precisely why the client's *conscious* mind hasn't been able to resolve the problem or create the kind of change they want. It's because, *subconsciously*, it isn't safe. The reason for this will be revealed through the process. But to gain access to that information, you must first prove to the subconscious mind that you can be trusted to safely guide the client through uncharted waters.

If you bump into "resistance" in a session, recognize that the subconscious mind is letting you know that it's not safe for the client to "go there" - *yet*. Before you attempt to go one step further in the process, you must first identify and then resolve the source of that resistance. In this way, you can walk the client right out of the problem.

---

[16] Radical Healing: Hypnosis Practitioner's Guide to Harnessing the Healing Power of the Educational Pre-Talk

Maintain the Relationship

Follow-up is a way to maintain the therapeutic relationship. That way should the client bump into a problem, or get triggered by something, they'll know what to do. They'll pick up the phone and call you. *Then* you can take care of it. This is the only sure way to ensure results that last.

The therapeutic relationship doesn't end once the client has achieved their goal. Send your clients and students an email from time to time. Check in with them to see how they're doing. Send them a birthday card. It only takes a few minutes to maintain the relationship. Your clients will love you for it.

Follow-up is how you ensure that your clients won't forget about you. They will remember you every time they meet someone who has a problem, and they'll refer you to friends and family and complete strangers. They'll come back to explore other issues they need help with.

Client Follow Up

When you complete a healing program, your client is no longer the same person. They have established a relationship of emotional intimacy with you. You *know* them. You have been through all the dark and empty places *with* them. You have shown that you *care* about their well-being. As a result, you've become a trusted friend and confidant. Care enough to keep the therapeutic contract open.

Your client lives in a world of people and things you know little about. Sometimes there can be triggers that you haven't dealt with. Most of the time it's because the person or situation that acts as a trigger wasn't a current concern while you were working on the issue. That person or situation simply wasn't present in your client's life at the time. As a result, they didn't come up. Then, the client goes back to daily living and three months, six months, a year down the road, something happens to trigger a recurrence of symptoms.

Some clients are going to need longer-term support. For example, a person with a significant amount of weight to lose will often benefit from having a follow-up session every three or four weeks. This helps to keep them motivated and accountable to their agreements while giving them the support they need to achieve their long-term goal. Sometimes that's all it takes.

Student Follow Up

Following up after you graduate a class keeps you top-of-mind. That will get you more business. You have just invested your time and energy into developing a rapport with a group of people. Don't just move onto the next project or the next group. You're building a tribe of hypnosis enthusiasts! Stay connected to your peeps. Show that you're there to support them should they have questions or need help.

Don't be shy about nagging them a little to keep up their practice. That just shows that you care about the results they're getting. Remember - you can't do it *for* them. All you can do is remind them that their goals and aspirations matter.

You can help your students to be successful by facilitating a monthly self-hypnosis practice group. This is a great way to maintain a loyal following. Each get-together provides you with another opportunity to reinforce the learning. It also gives you an opportunity to ask for referrals and/or upsell your students to private sessions.

Another easy way to keep people connected is to set up a group on social media. This is a great way to continue having a conversation with all your students on an ongoing basis.

If you're offering a group program or teaching an advanced class, offer your existing students a preferred rate. Better yet, offer them the program for free in exchange for hosting a class or signing up a friend. That's what I did. I taught a lot of classes using a hosting program.

Create a Referral Program

The hosting program I created rewarded people for taking on the task of promoting a class for me. In exchange for getting together 8 – 10 friends and family members for a class they received their course for free. Think Tupperware party. I provided them with everything they needed to promote the class to friends including ready-made email invitation text, posters, cards and brochures.

Who do you know that could benefit from learning a powerful self-empowerment, self-healing technique? Who else? Think outside the box. Yoga studios, healing centers, and churches often have space available. They also have an established client base to draw from and they're usually looking for additional sources of income.

Provide them with a promo kit and offer incentives. For example, you could offer to pay them a commission on a per-person enrollment basis for promoting your events. That's another win-win. What incentives could you offer a person for hosting your class or program?

Summary:

Your client relationship is a relationship based on trust. Your fundamental task is to make it safe for the client to follow your instructions. That's how you will achieve a lasting result.

Maintaining the relationship will help to ensure that your students and clients continue to enjoy all the benefits.

Having a client relationship system gives you a way to keep in touch with your clients and students. This helps to keep you top of mind which can generate repeat and referral business.

Having a client relationship system is a valuable part of your client attraction system. In an industry that is, too often, singularly motivated to just make the sale and move on, you can be different. Every time you connect with your clients, you remind them that you care, that they matter to you, that you're here to help. All they need to do is pick up the phone and call you. I've had clients book a session just to talk. They considered me a trusted friend and confidant; someone they felt safe with while bearing their soul. That's healing.

CHAPTER 11:
Grow Your Business

Too many hypnosis practices operate like turnstiles. They get a client in with a problem, do the session work, and then it's onto the business of getting the next client. From a purely practical point of view, it's very difficult to make a living offering one-off sessions. They don't tell you this in hypnosis school but, for most people, a single session just isn't going to get the job done. Sure, sometimes you get lucky. Sometimes you nail it in the first session. But I wouldn't count on it.

If all you do is get one client in for one session, you'll work too hard. You'll end up stuck in the rut of finding the next client just so you can pay the next bill. And you'll struggle to get consistent results working with the kinds of issues that people typically turn to hypnosis for help in resolving. What if there was a way to avoid the rut of chasing clients? What if there was a way you could deliver on your promise of results? What if you could get paid more for your valuable services?

Well, there is.

Unfortunately, most of us were only taught to think in terms of a single session. We were taught single-session protocols. For example, we learned a protocol for dealing with anxiety problems, another protocol for habit problems, and a protocol for addressing behavior problems. The problem with this approach is that no two clients are ever alike. People may come to you with similar issues, they may even present with the same symptoms, but it's never the same problem. This is because every problem is the result of a life experience.

The problem is always rooted in the client's life history - which is unique to them. That's why you'll get great results with one client and another client, with the same problem, won't respond to your techniques at all. In some cases, the problem can even get worse. This can leave you doubting yourself and your abilities.

It's not your fault. It's just that symptoms are seldom the whole problem. Symptoms are what tell a person that they *have* a problem. Often, they're just the tip of the iceberg. But you don't need more problems. You need a business system that will support you in delivering on your promise of results. That's what clients are paying for!

Hypnosis Practice Business System

The system I'm about to share with you gives both you and the client the time needed to ensure a lasting result. Not only can this help you to feel more confident working with more complex issues, but it can also get you out of the rut of getting one client in for one session. Consistently deliver on your promise of results and you'll naturally grow a referral-based business. As a result, you won't have to work so hard to make a living because you won't need as many clients.

The purpose of any system is to produce a specific result. Whether you're building a car, or a house, or a thriving healing practice, there's a series of steps involved in doing that. Picture an assembly line and you'll get the idea. The purpose of General Motor's assembly line is to produce a vehicle that works. That's the result they're after. If you want to brew a cup of coffee, there's a system. You put water in the machine. You put coffee in the filter. You put them all together and if you follow all the steps correctly, you'll have a freshly brewed cup of coffee to enjoy. If you want to build a house that you can live in, you need a plan to follow. You need a blueprint that shows you all the steps involved in building the house you want. The result is the design that suits you, that's the right fit for you. But the steps are always the same.

First, you prepare the ground because if you don't prepare the ground properly, you're going to have problems. You could end up with drainage problems or a sinking house. You don't want that! These are problems that can easily be avoided simply by following the blueprint. Next, you pour the foundation. If you skip a step, or try to cut corners on the foundation, you're going to have problems because, when things are not plumb or square at the foundation level, as you continue the building process, these problems become more exaggerated. You don't need problems. You need a solid foundation! The same is true of your hypnotherapy business.

The easiest way to understand the hypnosis practice business system is to think of it as a dating system. Both are centered on a relationship. Like dating, the relationship always begins with the 'attraction phase'. Then, there's the 'getting to know each other's phase. Then there's the 'first date,' which leads into going steady. And finally, marriage (which is where you and the client live happily ever after!)

Client Attraction

Client attraction is the first phase of the business system. Your goal is to attract clients you can be successful with. Your Who-What-How statement should attract people who are a match for your interests and qualifications. Remember, nobody cares about hypnosis. The only thing they care about is whether you can help them.

Also, the hypnosis market is highly saturated these days. Why compete when you can transcend? Most of the business is not in the surface stuff, anyway. It's in the deeper issues where nothing else has worked. That's when most people turn to alternative healing methods - usually as a last resort.

Surface issues are relatively easy to resolve. Typically, they require one to three sessions and have to do with skill development, symptom management, or behavioral improvements. For example, stress management and pain management are considered relatively simple issues because they respond well to surface techniques. Academic or sports improvement are often simple issues to resolve. Simple behavioral tweaks for issues like smoking and weight loss often respond well to simple techniques. But not always ... Even smoking and weight loss issues can turn out to be complex issues to deal with. Complex issues are emotional issues, and emotional issues can take time to resolve.

When you're dealing with an emotional issue, a surface approach will, at best, provide short-term relief. This is because there's an underlying emotion driving unwanted symptoms or behavior. If you fail to resolve what's driving the emotion, the client still has the problem. Sooner or later, the symptoms will return or be replaced by something worse.[17] This isn't to say that you can't make a living working only with surface issues. But if all that you're offering is relaxation therapy or symptom-management techniques, you've got plenty of competition. You need a way to distinguish yourself from the herd. You can do that by developing your knowledge and skill working with the deeper issues. That's where the business is waiting for you.

Everything you do to marketing yourself – from business cards, to websites, to social media presence, to giving presentations – is not to try to sell the session. It's to have a conversation. You need to have a conversation because not everyone is going to be the right fit for you. When you have that initial conversation, it's like going out for coffee for the first time. It's not a date. There's no commitment. You're just getting to know each other a little better.

Getting to Know Each Other

To deliver the best results to your clients, you need to feel confident in your sessions. The problem is that no two clients are alike. Some people are going to come to you with a simple issue that only requires a surface approach. Others are going to have more complex issues that require more time to resolve. Most people don't turn to hypnosis until they've tried everything else. As a result, by the time they turn to hypnosis, they're no longer dealing with a surface issue. Qualifying your clients ensures that you can feel confident moving forward with them. It will also get you a much higher success rate in your sessions.

---

[17] You can learn more about the Symptom Imperative in The Devil's Therapy: Hypnosis Practitioner's Essential Guide to Effective Regression Hypnotherapy.

Once you have qualified that a person is the right client for you, the next step is to get a commitment to the first session. Don't just pencil them in for an appointment! Use that initial conversation to get the client looking forward to their first session with you. Realize a lot can happen between the initial conversation and the first session. Some clients will get cold feet. This results in no-shows. You can prevent no-shows simply by telling the client what to expect in their first session with you. Not only does this help to get rid of any anticipatory fear, but it can also get your clients showing up for their first session feeling excited about working with you.

Here's what I tell my clients:

I call my first session a "Set for Success Session." The purpose of the first session is simply to assess. I want to have a look under the hood and see what we're dealing with. This will allow me to design a program that's best suited for you. There are three things that happen during that session.

First, we're going to talk. I'm going to ask you lots of questions. (That's your intake process.)

Second, I'm going to teach you what you need to know to be successful working with me. (That's your educational pre-talk.)

Third, I'm going to teach you how to relax into hypnosis. (Important keywords: "teach" and "relax.")

Talk: Notice how this is a client-centered approach. The client knows that nothing "bad" is going to happen. I'm not going to "technique" them or dump them into their stuff. I'm going to evaluate what their *needs* are before asking them to do anything. I'm going to let them tell me their tale of woe. This helps to establish trust. Besides, not every client is going to be ready for regression. Sometimes you'll need to do some preliminary work before you start guiding a client back into painful past events. But you won't know this until you have conducted the assessment.

Teach: The client also knows that I'm going to *teach* them what they need to know to be successful working with me. Hypnotherapy is an interactive process. The client must be willing to participate in their own healing process. This lets the client know that it's a learning process.

There's no need for concern about whether they can be hypnotized. Leave that to me! Now they can just be curious about what they might learn.

Relax: Finally, the last thing we're going to do is *relax* into hypnosis. A lot of people have fears about the hypnosis. Nobody is afraid to relax. After all, relaxation is hardly dangerous. Now, instead of getting all wound up about what might happen in the first session, the client can relax about the whole process.

Remember, this is the client's "first taste" of hypnosis with you. They don't really know what to expect. Even if they've experienced hypnosis with somebody else, this is their first experience with you. If you take care of all the unknowns ahead of time, you'll find that your clients are showing up for their first session feeling excited about having this opportunity to work with you. That's much better than feeling scared about what might happen, right?

Decide: Once you have explained what to expect in the first session, you can plant the seeds of expectation for a multi-session program by letting the client know that, following the first session, they can decide how they want to proceed with you. If they are obviously dealing with an emotional issue, I let the client know that they can continue on a per-session basis or sign up for a session package (which will save them a few bucks.) There's no need to decide anything, right now. The only thing you need right now is commitment to the first session.

Once you have the client booked in for their first session, send them written confirmation of their appointment. Some clients are pretty stressed out when they're talking to you over the phone, and stressed-out people forget things – including their appointment with you. Don't let that happen. If they don't show, you don't get paid.

Most people appreciate having things in writing. Not only is it professional, but this also helps to keep them committed. Include all the information they might need including the date and time of their appointment. If you work from home, include directions to make it easier to find you. Tell them where they can park. If they need a driver, do you have a waiting room? How long will their session be? Is there anything they can do to prepare for their first session. How can they pay you? What's your cancellation policy? Is there any paperwork you want them to complete before they come in? Make it easy for your clients to show up for their appointment. They'll thank you for it.

The First Date

The client's first session with you is like the first date. Officially this marks the beginning of the therapeutic relationship. Unfortunately, this is where a lot of healing practitioners are missing the boat. They use the first session to dive right into the client's issue, run into resistance, and don't know what to do. That can end up costing you your greatest asset in the session room - your confidence. You can use the client's first session in a more strategic way. For example, before the client shows up for their first session, I take a few minutes to prepare the space and make sure my client file is in order. I set out a glass of water for the client, check to make sure the bathroom is tidy and that there's enough toilet paper. Then, when the client arrives, I do exactly what I told the client would happen while we were booking the appointment.

First, we take care of business. I always get payment up front. Then, we take care of the preliminary paperwork before beginning the intake process. The intake process provides the information you need to guide the healing process. Remember, the client has this awful problem they've been struggling with. This is the reason they're seeing you. You need to listen. What you're listening for are important conscious and subconscious needs. Satisfying these needs *before* you induce hypnosis will result in there being much less resistance to deal with during the session.

I was taught, "Don't listen to the conscious mind! The conscious mind knows nothing!" That's partly true, but if you fail to satisfy the conscious mind's need to be heard, it has the power to block you. And the subconscious mind is never out of the picture. While you're listening to the client's story, the subconscious mind is watching *you*. It's listening to *you* and deciding whether it's safe to trust you. Listening demonstrates that you care enough to respect the needs of the client. This can get you a powerful rapport with the subconscious mind – and it knows where the bodies are buried!

Your first session should make your client a partner in the healing process. Hypnotherapy is not a passive process; it requires the client's participation. This is the purpose of your educational pre-talk – to establish the therapeutic contract. Some hypnosis practitioners start the first session with the pretalk, which is fine if all you're doing is a direct suggestion session. But for therapeutic hypnosis, need to start with the intake process because this gives you the information you need to make your pretalk relevant to the client's concerns and presenting issue. Remember, they're not paying you for the hypnosis. They're paying you for the result.

You do need to teach the client about hypnosis because that's what most people *think* they're paying for. But don't make a big deal about it. Keep the focus on the client's issue while identifying any fears or misconceptions the client might have so you can address them. Then, establish the therapeutic contract. You need that before you can proceed with the hypnosis. If you don't get it, you're going to have problems.

Once you have established the contract, you're ready to begin the hypnosis session. When you use the client's first hypnosis session to teach them how to work *with* you, your job becomes much easier. But before you start the induction, ask permission to begin. Most people think you're going to control them. Asking permission implies a choice. This can help to establish greater compliance – which will make your job easier.

In the first session, I always use a formal induction. A formal induction is a ritual with a clear beginning and a clear ending. This helps to satisfy the client's need to know that they were hypnotized. I also verify that they're in hypnosis. Before emerging the client from hypnosis, I use a convincer to prove to them that the hypnosis happened. Remember, they're invested in hypnosis being the answer. Let them know that they got what they paid for! I then use a formal emerging count.

If you use the client's first experience of hypnosis with you to teach them how to work with you within the context of a safe environment, you'll remove the fear of the unknown. Even if they dive into some painful feelings, they'll discover that it's safe to allow those feelings.

They'll know that it's safe to let you guide them through the process. You'll also get a good idea of what you're dealing with before diving into the deeper work of unresolved feelings and memories. Subsequent sessions will then be part of a more organic process, each providing the next logical step in the client's healing program.

Now, look at what you have just accomplished. You have:

1. Assessed the client's readiness for the deeper work
2. Satisfied important conscious and subconscious needs
3. Made your client a partner in a healing program
4. Taught the client how to work with you as a partner in a therapeutic relationship
5. Identified the next step in the client's healing program.

That's a lot of mileage for a single session! Not only that! You're now set up to facilitate a multi-session healing program. Multiple session clients will teach you more about healing than any classroom training ever could. Experience will help you to grow your confidence and skill, allowing you to take on more complex issues. As a result, you'll be able to help more people. This is where the business is at. It's in the more complex issues. Over time, you'll develop a kind of radar. You'll notice things more quickly. You'll pick up on patterns and clues. You'll recognize stuff that you used to overlook, and you'll be able to respond more quickly and effectively. This can help you to carve out a niche for yourself that's based on your unique interests and skill set. That's when you can start charging more for your services.

It's just a matter of time. Emotional issues often take more time to resolve because they have roots in traumatic memory. Regression hypnotherapy is highly effective for resolving the uncomfortable thoughts and feelings associated with traumatic memories. Because most people are resistant to facing uncomfortable memories, regression hypnotherapy is not a single session approach. Some hypnosis practitioners are intimidated by regression work. Some have been taught that regression is "bad" or "damaging" or "retraumatizing." What they fail to realize is that clients will regress whether you want them to or not - often when you least expect it! And surface techniques won't work for deeper issues. Not for long, at least.

If your goal is to deliver a *lasting* result to your client, you're going to need to develop your skill working with emotional issues. Then use the first session to prepare the client for the healing journey. Using your first session to kick off a healing program will give you the time you need to assess and prepare your client for the healing process.

Based on the information provided by the client, you can then plan the next best step for that client. Remember, you can't make a person heal. All you can do is guide the process. It takes consciousness to heal consciousness. Some clients are going to need more time to allow healing to happen.

Going Steady

Once you decide to continue working together, this is where your multi-session system begins. Now you're dating. When a client commits to a healing program, it's like you're going steady. This will give you and the client the time you need to ensure a lasting result. Remember, clients don't pay you to hypnotize them. They pay you to help them lose the weight, break the habit, heal the relationship, and put an end to the pain. These things can take time because nothing is going to happen without the client's consent. Multiple sessions give the client enough time to both allow change to happen, and to integrate change between sessions.

When you're dealing with an emotional issue, it's seldom going to be a quick fix. There's always resistance to facing uncomfortable feelings because they don't feel good! There can be multiple factors contributing to the client's problem. Sometimes, you can be dealing with a constellation of issues working together. These things take time to be brought to light and resolved.

If you want a sure-fire way to get lasting results from your session-work, test the results between sessions. Whatever happens between sessions will tell you what the next step in the client's healing process needs to be. Realize, change doesn't happen during the session – it happens after the client leaves the session. That's when post-hypnotic suggestions take effect.

Marriage

When you help a person to achieve their goal you end up married to them. You have a client who knows you and trusts you. They've shared things with you that they've never told another living soul. They will refer to you as "my hypnotherapist." You're in a committed relationship. This is how you grow a referral-based business – deliver on your promise of results.

When you retire a client, schedule them in for a 30-day follow-up session, just to be sure. Keeping the contract open means that, if there's something you missed, or a deeper layer comes to consciousness, you'll get the opportunity to take care of it. This is yet another way to ensure a lasting result. If their follow-up session reveals that the problem is really gone for good, you can then use that session to reward the client for all their good work. In this case, give them a really yummy experience to polish things off. They deserve it! Make it a memorable experience of celebrating change. Encourage your client to own their accomplishments. They did that!

Even when you're confident that the issue has been completely resolved, you never know. Keeping the "marriage" contract open also allows you to continue to test the results in the client's daily life. Some clients can bump into unexpected triggers months later. Some may experience a recurrence of symptoms. Let them know that, should something happen, it's not a failure. It's not a failure. It's just how the mind works.

Some people are going to need ongoing support. Scheduling them in for regular follow-up sessions can help them to achieve a long-term goal. Teach them techniques that they can use on their own to be more successful. For example, self-hypnosis, breathwork, tapping.

Every client you help is potentially a long-term client because they will come back to see you for other issues. This makes the final phase in the business system part of your client-attraction system because these clients will become a source of referrals. They'll send you their friends and family members to help. They'll even refer you to strangers. I know this because I've had clients referred to me by psychiatrists, counselors, psychologists, and people I have never met. And it's because one of my clients was their patient, or sister, or cousin, or mother.

The easiest way to grow your healing practice is to let other people do it for you. Being recommended by a trusted friend will bring you clients who don't need any further convincing. They'll be your best clients, ever.

That's really the purpose of your client attraction system. It's to speak directly to your ideal client in a way that gets them to call you. And your best client attractor – bar none – is a client who has become a raving fan.

An Integrated Practice-Business System

You have everything you need, right now, to begin creating a simple business plan for your practice. This is the system that worked for me to get more consistent results working with a variety of issues. It can help you, too. It's easy to understand because there are just five steps. It's easy to duplicate because, like dating, it's based on a relationship.

1. First, comes the attraction phase …
2. Then there's the getting to know each other phase …
3. Then there's the first date …
4. Which leads to going steady …
5. And finally, marriage, which is where you and the client live happily ever after.

Take the time to think about these five interconnected systems and how you can use this blueprint to grow your healing practice. The steps are always going to be the same but how you apply them may require some customization to get the best fit for you. Your system should support you in doing your best work. Just follow the blueprint. Find what works best for you.

So that's it.

You now have some simple strategies you can use to grow your healing practice. The business side is how you make a living as a healing practitioner. This begins with client attraction because you need clients to make a living. The practice side is what happens in the session room once you have attracted a client.

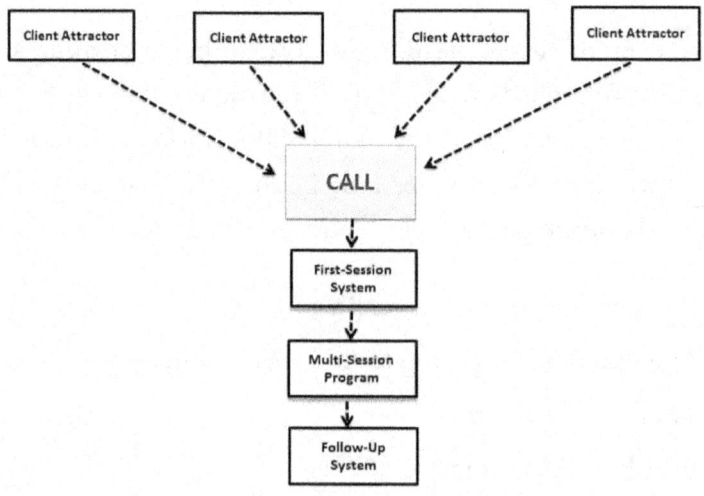

Having a system to support you in your sessions with clients will help you to do your best work. Having a multi-session system can help you to get better, more consistent results working with a variety of client issues. Not only will your results increase your confidence

which will support you in taking on more challenging issues. Your reputation for delivering on your promise of results will bring you referrals – so you won't have to work so hard to make a living.

Ready to learn more?

The Devil's Therapy: *Hypnosis Practitioner's Essential Guide to Effective Regression Hypnotherapy.* Discover how a 200-year-old fairy tale reveals a complete system for facilitating effective regression hypnotherapy. Learn the "Why" behind the "How-To" of regression to cause hypnosis. Turn your hypnosis sessions into healing programs and get results that last. This practical guidebook gives you a step-by-step map you can use to facilitate successful regression therapy. It's much simpler than you might imagine.

This is absolutely amazing work. It's so clear and precise, just like a laser. It leaves no doubts about what to do, how to do it, and the best part: Why to do it!! - **Zoran Pavlovic, Belgrade, Serbia**

The Devil's Therapy provides a simple three-phase, seven-step protocol for facilitating regression to cause therapeutic hypnosis. The first phase is comprised of three steps which effectively set up for a multi-session healing program. The second phase is comprised of two steps which make up the core work of regression to cause and inner child work. The third phase involves the final two steps of testing/integrating all changes followed by the forgiveness work.

Available on Amazon in English, German, and French versions.

Ditch the Script: *Get Everything You Need from the Client for Successful Hypnotherapy and Set Up to Wrap Up with Results.* Your success is always going to be in your set up. Ditch the Script reveals simple strategies you can use right away to break free of 'scriptnotism' and start facilitating client-centered regression to cause therapeutic hypnosis. Learn how to qualify your clients, conduct the strategic intake process, and more.

Available on Amazon

I read the first chapter before bed. Wow! Really good! Can't wait to absorb this book!! I didn't think anything could top the first book. After reading one chapter of this second book. I was clearly wrong! – **Michael Madden, USA**

Radical Healing: *Hypnosis Practitioner's Guide to Harnessing the Healing Power of the Educational Pretalk.* Learn how to prepare your clients for a body-centered approach to healing the mind. Discover how every phase of the healing process involves a contract – from the initial call with a prospective client, to the first session, for the hypnosis, and for regression.

Available on Amazon

Wendie's lessons have been invaluable in helping me to understand the subconscious mind and I feel like I really get it now. I used what I learned right away to great effect with my clients, and it has taken my practice to a whole new level of learning. My clients are seeing results faster! The insights and healing just come more naturally, now – it just seems to flow easily. – **Craig Homonnay, Australia**

The Devil's Little Black Book: *Regression Hypnotherapist's Troubleshooting Guide with Tips, Tricks & Even Scripts to Tweak Your Therapeutic Technique.* Where *The Devil's Therapy* answers the question, "Why do we do what we do when we do it?" *The Devil's Little Black Book* answers the question, "What if?" What if sh*t happens in a session and you don't know what to do? This companion guide to *The Devil's Therapy* provides proven strategies for dealing with some of the more predictable ways resistance can show up in your sessions with client – and what to do when it does.

Available on Amazon

After almost 40 years of doing hypnosis, I discovered your phenomenal books and online videos very recently and it opened up the floodgates of memories in my career. Your history of hypnotherapy, your trials and tribulations, parallel mine . . . I am going to recommend your books to all those people who've been bugging me to put to paper these principles. I wish I had heard of you years before when I was active, and an industry turned against me because I refused to take shortcuts and jump on the latest bandwagon of change-work for the month. – **John Petrocelli, USA**

Ditch the Pitch!

Dream Healing Practitioner Guidebook: *A Healer's Guide to Uncovering the Secret Messages of Your Dreams*. Learn deceptively simple techniques you can use – yourself and with others – to uncover the meaning of your dreams. If you're a healing practitioner, *Dream Healing* gives you an insight therapy you can offer to clients. *Dream Healing* can help you to develop valuable skills that can support you in your healing sessions with clients. Working with your own dreams can help you to develop intuition while bringing balance and harmony to your mind-body system.

Available on Amazon

Makes Things So Simple

I have thoroughly loved working with dream healing tools. Wendie makes things so simple and easy that learning new skills such as dream healing become easy to apply and implement from the start. I have absolutely loved uncovering my dream meanings and then putting what I've learnt into action because understanding a dream is not enough; it also needs some change/action for resolution to happen. It's been such an interesting and fun experience. Thank you, so much! – **Nicole Dodd, UK**

Ready for Regression: *Hypnosis Practitioner's Guide to Preparing Clients for Effective Regression Hypnotherapy.* The Ready for Regression First Session System is based on a five-star rated course. Gain the confidence you need to guide your clients through the multiple healing processes of Regression to cause therapeutic hypnosis.

> *IT WORKS!!!! I just finished a NEW session with a NEW client located in Asia. I had my semi-completed session manual with me that I put together based on your training course and . . . wow. It works. Confidence was back. Client felt great. Deep trance. I could go on forever. In short - thank you, Wendie. I put your course and method to real life and IT WORKS!!!!!! It works!!!! A huge suffocating hug to you!!! Thank you!!! And I didn't even complete all the courses yet!!!*
>
> *~ Jo Nontakorn*

Get clear. Get confident. Get ready!

Wendie Webber

With over thirty years of experience as a healing practitioner, Wendie brings a broad range of skills to her unique approach to regression to cause hypnosis.

She is an Omni-Hypnosis graduate, 5-Path practitioner, Transactional hypnotherapist, Alchemical hypnotherapist, Satir Transformational Systemic therapist, and Regression Hypnotherapy Boot Camp participant.

Before hypnosis, Wendie owned a self-help bookstore where she explored spirituality, psychology, and energy-based healing.

Wendie is the recipient of the 2006 5-PATH Leadership Award and the 2019 Gerald F. Kein OMNI Award for Excellence in Hypnotism.

She enjoys an eclectic lifestyle on Vancouver Island, British Columbia, Canada, surrounded by nature, oracles, and cats.

The Devil's Therapy Series

Book 1: The Devil's Therapy: *Hypnosis Practitioner's Essential Guide to Effective Regression Hypnotherapy*

Book 2: Ditch the Pitch: *Simple Proven Client Attraction Strategies for Hypnosis Practitioners Who Don't Love Digital Marketing*

Book 3: Ditch the Script: *Get Everything You Need from the Client for Successful Hypnotherapy and Set Up to Wrap Up with Results*

Book 4: Radical Healing: *Hypnosis Practitioner's Guide to Harnessing the Healing Power of the Educational Pretalk*

Book 5: The Devil's Little Black Book: *Regression Hypnotherapist's Troubleshooting Guide with Tips, Tricks & Even Scripts to Tweak Your Therapeutic Technique*

Book 6: The Dream Healing Practitioner Guidebook: *A Healer's Guide to Uncovering the Secret Messages of Your Dreams*

Book 7: Ready for Regression: *Hypnosis Practitioner's Guide to Preparing Clients for Effective Regression Hypnotherapy*

www.ingramcontent.com/pod-product-compliance
Lightning Source LLC
Chambersburg PA
CBHW070605010526
44118CB00012B/1451